WALKING IN THE SIERRA NEVADA
SPAIN

Boca de la Pesca from Cerro de las Pipas. (Baja Montaña Route 1)

WALKING IN
THE SIERRA NEVADA
SPAIN

by

ANDY WALMSLEY

CICERONE PRESS
MILNTHORPE, CUMBRIA

ACKNOWLEDGEMENTS

Many people have helped me with the preparation of this guide, but I would especially like to thank the following: Professor Antonio Echarri, for hospitality, interest and local knowledge; Tim Kelly, for drawing much better maps than I could have managed; Ian Roberts, Glyn Denver and Keith Denver, for accompanying me on my various trips, tolerating my dogged determination to sniff out sometimes obscure routes, and also for the use of their photographs; Laurence Siedler for local information; and, last but not least, my parents, for their support, encouragement, and their belief in my ability to complete the project.

Front Cover: Approaching Pico de la Carne from the north-east

CONTENTS

PART 2: BAJA MONTAÑA (LOW MOUNTAINS)

PART 3: ALTA MONTAÑA (HIGH MOUNTAINS)

PREFACE

When I first discovered the Sierra Nevada in the mid-1980s I was surprised that the range was so little known in Britain. Here were mountains of over 11,000 feet, the highest surpassing any in the Pyrenees. Here was a climate which embraced summer temperatures of over 100 degrees Fahrenheit, and winter ones which can dip well below freezing, giving one of the most extreme summer/winter contrasts to be found anywhere. Here was a first-class ski-resort which was (then) completely unknown to British skiers. Here was the highest road in Europe, surpassing all the famous alpine passes. Here was a veritable adventure playground for mountain-bikers and 4-wheel-drive enthusiasts. And here was solitude. Despite the development of the ski-resort (then called Sol y Nieve - 'sun and snow') and track building in many valleys, this comparatively small area could - and still can -provide that wilderness experience now so sadly lacking in other European ranges.

It was obvious that these mountains were crying out for a guidebook on the lines of Kev Reynolds' *Walks and Climbs in the Pyrenees*, which was a prized possession of mine. I commenced work on the guide in August 1991, and spent the following 2½ years exploring the range thoroughly, including many hours pouring over maps and burning the midnight word-processor. This is the result.

Andy Walmsley, 1995

INTRODUCTION

The mountains of Spain's Sierra Nevada have been largely ignored by British mountaineers and walkers. With attractions such as the Alps and Pyrenees closer at hand, few have penetrated far enough south to discover these wild and barren peaks.

With massive overcrowding and exploitation of the Alps, and increasingly of the Pyrenees too, many walkers and climbers are eagerly searching out new stamping grounds. Areas in which to recapture the solitude and sense of adventure now found lacking among the more popular ranges. The Sierra Nevada can provide this experience.

It would be wrong to portray the range as a wilderness, however. On the north-western slopes, overlooking the city of Granada, there has been considerable development, with the building of a large ski-resort and all the gubbins which go with it. On these slopes also is a tarmac road to the summit of Pico del Veleta - the highest road in Europe.

Despite this, it is still easy to find solitude among these mountains. Stray a kilometre or two from the Sierra Nevada road and other humans become a rare sight, even on the 'frequented' routes. On some of the more remote ridges it is not unusual to observe 'cabra montés' (a relative of the Pyrenean ibex) at close quarters, but you would have to have your camera very handy to photograph them; their speed and agility over rough terrain is breathtaking.

The nature of these mountains is quite unlike the more famous ranges further north; there are no Matterhorns or Pic du Midis here. The striking thing about the high Sierrra Nevada is the sense of space and the impression of vast scale, something which is difficult to capture on a photograph and which really needs to be experienced first-hand. At first glance, the range could be compared to England's Helvellyn range or Scotland's Grey Corries, but closer acquaintance is more likely to remind one of the Cuillin of Skye without the mist! Comparisons are futile, though; these peaks have a unique character all their own. Although lacking the spectacular peaks of the Alps, there are profound corries ('corrals') beneath the 600m north faces, jagged and pinnacled ridges, and tiny jewel-like tarns to please the most jaundiced eye.

TOPOGRAPHY

The Sierra Nevada takes the form of a long curved ridge some 100km in length. Commencing in the east in the vicinity of Almería it gains height gradually, only attaining its culminating altitude of 3482m quite close to Granada before subsiding relatively rapidly into the plains of La Vega, to the south-west of that city.

Most of the interesting peaks (and all the '3000-ers') are concentrated in the 55km between the passes of La Ragua in the east and Suspiro del Moro in the west, the so-called High Sector. It is this section which is covered by this guide.

Walking west from the Puerto de la Ragua, the traveller first passes over an undulating section of broad ridge, taking in the summits of Morron, San Juan, Peñon del Puerto and Cerro Trevélez, all these tops reaching an altitude of between 2700 and 2900m. The ridge then reaches the foot pass of Puerto de Trevélez (*c.*2800m) before rising to Cerro Pelao, the first of the 3000-ers, with 3000m spurs branching north and south.

The main ridge continues, curving gradually southwards and passes over a number of minor summits, all conflictingly labelled on various Spanish maps, before reaching the second major foot pass, the Cuneta de Vacares (2974m). The terrain, hitherto merely bouldery, now becomes craggy as the ridge narrows and rises abruptly to the sharp peaks of Vacares and Goterón. The ridge now makes two big climbs and descents, traversing Alcazaba and Mulhacén with the Cañada de las Siete Lagunas in between, before turning westwards across the jagged crests of Puntal de la Caldera and Crestones de Rio Seco.

Another pronounced rise leads to the summit of Los Machos, the shattered and pinnacled ridge, then proceeding via an abrupt rock step to the summit of Veleta, the second highest peak of the range. From here, a number of lesser ridges radiate north and north-west, carrying the peaks of Baja Montaña or low mountains, along with the Sierra Nevada Road and ski-resort. The main ridge veers gradually south-west over the rocky summits of Virgen and Neveros to the Elorietta hut at the head of the Lanjarón valley.

The ridge now divides to embrace the valley, the eastern arm carrying only one further 3000m peak, Pico del Tajo de Los Machos, before descending gradually to the Alpujarras. The western arm continues over the rocky tops of Tosal de Cartujo and Tajos Altos to the final 3000-er (Cerro del Caballo), and then rapidly descends to the spa town of Lanjarón.

From this main spine ridges ('lomas') and valleys project like ribs, the northerly ones draining into the valley of the Genil, the southerly ones descending to the Alpujarras region, the streams feeding the Rio Guadalfeo. The southern valleys take the form of long narrow ravines, the most famous being the Poqueira, which contains the enchanting moorish villages of Capileira, Bubión and Pampaneira. The northern valleys are much wilder, with no access by car, and culminate in the spectacular corrals beneath the towering crags of the north faces.

Thus, the area of the guide is conveniently bounded, in the west by the N323 road over the pass of Suspiro del Moro, in the east by the C331 over Puerto de la Ragua, to the north by the valley of the Rio Genil, and to the south by the Rio Guadalfeo.

CLIMATE

Generally, the Sierra Nevada enjoys a settled climate, with weather conditions which are relatively predictable. July and August are the driest, warmest and most snow-free months and during this period clear and sunny weather can be virtually guaranteed.

It may seem strange to be talking of 'snow-free' periods when discussing a range of peaks lying only 70km from all the all-year warmth of the Costa del Sol, but the climate changes rapidly as one travels north from the coast. The mountains, of course, play a major role in these climatic variations, serving as a barrier which protects the Costa from the extreme variations of the central meseta.

In the area around Granada, winters can be very cold with night time temperatures below freezing. Add 3000m of altitude, and the winds which go with it, and you are into a climate of arctic blizzards and cold. It is essential for winter 'Sierristas' to provide themselves with equivalent equipment and clothing to the Scottish winter climber or alpinist.

Due to the fact that the bulk of the snowfall occurs between October and February, the prime winter mountaineering season is late March to mid May when the snow will be more consolidated and there is a good chance of that magical combination of blue skies

11

and dazzling white peaks.

By late May the thaw or 'deshielo' - literally de-icing - is well underway as temperatures rise inexorably, and by July the snowy landscape which gave the range its name has become a sun-baked and barren semi-desert.

During the summer the temperatures on the high summits on a fine day are ideal for walking in shorts and tee-shirt, with temperatures in the low 20s Celsius and an ever-present breeze, but the weather can change quite suddenly, making it essential to carry extra weather-proof clothing.

Ascents of the lower peaks - Baja Montaña - can be gruelling during July and August when valley temperatures soar to more than 40°C, but these mountains make excellent winter outings, a light cover of snow often dusting their summits.

By mid September the settled weather usually begins to break down, with more chance of cloud cover and lower temperatures, leading into the wetter and colder period when most of the snowfall occurs. October and November are the most unpredictable months; during late October and early November 1993 there was rain and cloud almost every day, with only short sunny intervals.

Settled periods do occur during winter, however - the Christmases of both 1991 and 1992 were brilliantly sunny and clear, producing ideal conditions for skiing, mountaineering, or walking.

The January-February period brings the most extreme weather of the year with brilliant blue skies or blizzards equally likely, and much avalanche danger on the high peaks. The pattern begins to settle again by mid March, leading back into the long hot summer.

FLORA AND FAUNA

The combination of high altitude and southerly latitude endows the Sierra Nevada with a rich variety of plant and animal life, some species being unique to this range. The huge range of climates, from semi-tropical in the summer valleys, to near-arctic on the winter summits, means that the diversity of flora and fauna is unequalled anywhere else in Europe.

The Zona Alta or high zone, ostensibly barren, contains a surprising wealth of life during the summer months, with tiny patches of colour springing up around the 'lagunas' and 'ventisqueros' (tarns and snowpatches). Various flowers, such as the Nevada daffodil and Nevada crocus, are found only in this area of Spain. Insects, too, are numerous, and the larger varieties will bring a shudder or two from folk of a nervous disposition; some of the flying insects look and sound like particularly well armed helicopter gunships!

Rather more pleasant are the numerous butterflies which flutter constantly around your feet as you walk along some of the more remote ridges. One of them, the Nevada blue, is found only here and in the Pyrenees.

Capra Pyrenaica Hispánica, a type of ibex locally known simply as 'cabra montés' (mountain goat), can be found throughout the Sierra, but obviously prefer the quieter areas. They are most easily seen during the evening on the lower peaks, when a quiet sit down on a lonely summit can be rewarded with remarkably close encounters with these majestic creatures.

Bird life is also varied and abundant. Besides the expected mountain birds such as choughs, golden eagles and alpine accentors, it is surprising to encounter species from further north such as blackbird and greenfinch, which find a replica of more northerly climates on the slopes of these high hills.

The lower slopes and peaks of the range have sparse forests of pine, holm oak, olive, chestnut and poplar, but the chief feature of the 1600-2100m band is the prickly ground shrubs. There are various species, some of which look surprisingly harmless, but they have spines which can penetrate soft walking boots with ease, and which are very painful if inadvertently used as a handhold. This altitude band is sometimes called the 'zona erizo' (hedgehog zone).

In the valleys, the abundance of water from the melting snows and the ideal climate allows the cultivation of all manner of exotic fruits, including plums, apricots, oranges, figs, custard-apples and, of course, grapes. In the fertile plain of La Vega to the west of Granada, it is not unusual to grow three crops per year.

FOOD AND DRINK

The Spanish, like the Italians and the French, are great food lovers, and think nothing of spending two hours or more over a meal, with vast amounts of food, wine and conversation. This could perhaps account for the fact that the mountains are often deserted; something as trivial as climbing mountains must never be allowed to interfere with eating or the 'siesta'.

However, tempting though the Spanish lifestyle is, it is necessary for the dedicated mountaineer to strike a balance between time spent out on the hill and time indulging in the culinary pleasures of Andalucia.

The range of supermarket foods available in Spain is very much on a par with Britain, including prices but alcoholic drinks are very much cheaper. For example, a 1 litre carton of local table wine in a Granada supermarket was 80 pesetas (about 45p) in October 1993, while a box of twenty-four 33cl bottles of 'cerveza' (beer) was priced at 750 pesetas (less than 18p per bottle). It is more expensive to drink Coke than beer in Spain. Bottled mineral water (carbonated 'con gas' and still 'sin gas') is popular - particularly the Lanjarón 'Agua de Sierra Nevada' - and prices are similar to those in the UK.

Spanish bread (even better than the more famous French), cheese, spicy sausages like 'chorizo' and 'salsichon', 'morcilla' (like a spiced black pudding), and 'gazpacho' (a cold tomato and garlic soup) all make good cheap ingredients of an appetising camp kitchen.

So, camping and self-catering is still relatively cheap, but eating out can be costly, depending on where you choose to eat. City centre restaurants are as expensive as the British variety, but there are some excellent bars out in the villages and tucked away in the Sierra where a superb meal can be had for a pittance.

Specially recommended are the Bar Chiquito in the Genil valley where they make superb 'patatas a lo pobre' (poor potatoes) - sliced potatoes fried with herbs and garlic - and the Merendero de la Fuente del Hervidero on the Huenes valley forestry road, where a wealth of superb local dishes is available. Among these is 'conejo' (rabbit - a great favourite in Spain), and local 'salsichas' (spicy sausages) often served with 'orgaza' (a large flat loaf of crusty bread). Both these establishments (and there are many others) are unpretentious places - some might even say scruffy - but serve excellent, satisfying meals at very low prices.

Without willpower it is easy to spend most of your time indulging in sampling the Spanish cuisine and very little climbing mountains.

ACCESS

BY AIR

Although Granada has its own airport, it does not take international flights (though there are plans to upgrade it for the 1996 World Alpine Ski Championships). The nearest international airports at present are at Málaga and Almería, both situated about 150km (90 miles) from Granada. Málaga is the largest of the two, and being the main Costa del Sol destination means it has a large number of flights available from most UK airports. Prices vary widely but there are many bargain flights to be had, and flying to the Costa will usually prove cheaper than most other European destinations.

Buses from either airport to Granada are frequent. From Málaga via Loja or Motril, and from Almería via Guadix. If your intention is to reach the Alpujarras rather than the Granada region, then the best option would be a flight to Málaga, then by bus to Motril. From Motril a bus may be caught to the Alpujarran centres of Lanjarón or Orgiva.

Car hire is readily available at the airports and is undoubtedly the most convenient way to explore the Sierra Nevada, if not the cheapest. To use some of the more remote roads within the Sierra, a 4-wheel-drive (4WD) type vehicle is preferable and these can be hired also, but prices are approximately double those for a Ford Fiesta or SEAT Marbella. Car hire costs about the same in Spain as in the UK.

BY TRAIN

The drawback of using trains to travel to southern Spain is the condition of the Spanish national railway network (R.E.N.F.E.). British Rail seems positively futuristic by comparison, and the French TGV something from science fiction. Despite some isolated exceptions (notably the Costa del Sol railway) the Spanish trains leave a lot to be desired.

BY COACH

Various companies run direct coach trips to Granada. Check your local bus station's information office. Prices vary, but this seems the cheapest - if least comfortable - way for an individual to get to the Sierra Nevada.

BY CAR

For a family or group of three or more people, driving will prove the most cost-effective way of travelling to the Sierra, and has the added advantage of having the convenience of your own vehicle during your stay. The nature of the Sierra Nevada makes a vehicle highly desirable for the explorer with limited holiday time. This is the author's preferred means of access, but the Sierra Nevada is a very long way south, and not everyone is such a fanatical motorist as the author.

There are a number of route options, regarding both ferries and roads. Brittany Ferries offer the tempting 24 hour crossing from Plymouth to Santander, and P&O run a Portsmouth to Bilbao service, both of these cutting out the crossing of France altogether, saving between 500 and 600 miles of driving and offering a direct route across Spain via Burgos and Madrid. Its disadvantages are the comparative infrequency of sailings and high cost (approximately double the cost of shorter sailings with the same lines).

More reasonably priced (and more frequent) sailings are available from Brittany Ferries, Sealink and P&O to a number of ports on the Brittany/Normandy coast, from which good roads will take you south into Spain, either directly, via Bayonne, or scenically, via the Pyrenees - a convenient overnight stop. If crossing the Pyrenees, the optimum route goes south via Bordeaux and Pau, crosses the mountains via the Pourtalet (scenic) or Somport (easier) passes, and traverses Spain via Huesca, Zaragoza and Madrid on excellent roads.

For any of these routes a sensible timescale for the traveller who is making directly for the Sierra is a day each for crossing France and Spain, plus an appropriate allowance for travelling to the British ferry port. France can be crossed quickly but expensively if pay ('peage') Autoroutes are used, or more slowly on the free 'Routes Nationales'. Spain now has first-class free 'Autovias' (dual carriageways, as good as the toll 'Autopistas' on the east side of the country) and these will take you all the way from Zaragoza to Bailen, bypassing Madrid en route.

VALLEY BASES

The choice of low bases is wide, and the decision as to which suits you will depend on your own preferences. Camping or hotels, lively or quiet, modern or with a sense of history.

GRANADA is the biggest city in the area (pop. 275,000) and is very convenient for the north and west of the Sierra. Granada can be very busy and hotel accommodation within the city will only suit those who are determined to enjoy the cultural sights and the nightlife of the old moorish capital.

Access to the Sierra Nevada Road and the Genil valley is obviously easy. There is at least one bus up to 3200m (snow permitting) on the Veleta road each day.

Access to the southern side of the range is also possible by bus to Lanjarón or Orgiva, but if you really want to savour the atmosphere of the Alpujarras you must stay in one of the villages.

The two main villages mentioned above both boast a range of hotels (Lanjarón has 24), but quieter and more evocative centres are to be found in the striking Poquiera ravine where the moorish settlements of Pampaneira, Bubión, and Capileira cling to the eastern slopes of the valley. The unmade section of the Sierra Nevada Road starts just above Capileira, and from here, it is possible to drive almost to the summit of Spain, Mulhacén, at 3482m. Based at Pampaneira is the guiding company Nevadensis S.C.A., which runs a range of guided tours of the Sierra on foot, on horeseback, in 4WD vehicles, and in combinations of all three (address & phone no. in Appendix A).

Further east in the Alpujarras lies the highest village in Spain, Trevélez, which straddles the 1500m contour. There is an excellent campsite here, as well as small hotels, and many superb walks commence from the village, including the traditional route up Mulhacén.

The many delectable villages in the eastern Alpujarras, such as Juviles, Mecina Bombarón, and Yegen, are interesting, but do not make good bases for the routes on the high peaks unless a vehicle is available as they are rather remote from the usual starting points.

Along the western fringe of the range, adjacent to the main Granada-Motril road, lie a number of small towns such as Durcal and Padul, but these have little to recommend them as bases. In this

17

vicinity only the hamlet of Nigüelas stands out as a pleasant place; its tiny Plaza de la Iglesia with central fountain is exquisite.

The area surrounding Granada itself has numerous small villages which make excellent bases. The best of these is undoubtedly La Zubia, close to the city, and ideally placed for the exploration of Baja Montaña. La Zubia boasts a good second category campsite (Reina Isabel), hotels, bars, shops, and even an outdoor pursuits club - Club Deportiva de La Zubia.

Also worthy of mention are the villages of Huetor Vega, and Monachil. The former is a busy little place, with lively bars. Monachil, by contrast, is tucked away in a deep valley, and is a jumble of buildings clustered around narrow streets on the banks of the Rio Monachil. This river has an eventful life on its way to the village. Its source lies high under the summit of Veleta, and its upper reaches pass through the Sierra Nevada ski-resort, serving as one of the centre's best known 'pistas' (El Rio) in winter. Lower down, the river is utilised for hydro-electrical purposes, and finally, just above the village, it plunges through Los Cahorros, a spectacular gorge containing some awesome cliffs where rock climbing at the highest grades is practised.

On the eastern side of Granada commences the Sierra Nevada Road, its initial stretch passing through the villages of Cenes and Pinos Genil (many hotels on this road). Just before the bridge over the Genil, a road branches left to Güéjar Sierra, and towards the upper Genil valley. The large village of Güéjar possesses all amenities (including a 'Discoteca'!) and is well placed for the exploration of the Genil and its upper 'barrancos'. Just before the village, the road passes the Las Lomas campsite, which is first category and highly recommended, having the usual facilities (swimming pool, shop, restaurant, etc), and an affable owner who speaks a little English. The site offers discounts for 7 day and 10 day stays out of season and runs guided trips (during summer) into the Sierra both on foot and on horseback.

Further details of some of these bases are given in the introductions to the particular areas.

The above is by no means a comprehensive list of all possible valley bases; it is merely a selection of those which in the author's experience represent the most convenient. Enterprising readers may discover their own favourites - there are certainly other possibilities.

MOUNTAIN BASES

SIERRA NEVADA SKI CENTRE

The purpose-built ski-resort was originally given the name Sol y Nieve (Sun and Snow), an appropriate title considering the climate, but this has now been dropped in favour of the more prosaic Sierra Nevada. It was decided that the name Sol y Nieve would not be readily understood on publicity material during the run-up to the 1996 World Alpine Ski Championships. Locally, the actual complex is referred to by the name of the hollow in which it is built - Prado Llano - which translates loosely as 'flat pastures'. During the summer, these one time pastures look more like quarry workings, the ski-lift paraphernalia, bulldozed pistas and jumbled square buildings being depressingly unattractive. The centre is not actually closed in summer - there are usually at least two hotels open - but it tends to have a closed-season atmosphere, with many shuttered bars and restaurants. The location of the centre close to Veleta and the Sierra Nevada Road, make it a convenient base, but between May and November it is a rather dreary one.

As with all ski-resorts, however, winter presents a quite different perspective, with the bustling centre surrounded by dazzling white slopes, usually swarming with a multi-coloured melée of skiers. If this kind of lively scene appeals, then you will not be disappointed with Prado Llano in winter. If you prefer solitude, then other areas are obviously preferable.

The ski area occupies the head of the Monochil valley, which descends north-west from the summit of Veleta between the Loma de Dilar and the knobbly ridge of the Peñones de San Francisco, extending almost to the 3394m summit itself. Prado Llano clings to the eastern slopes of this hollow (between 2100 and 2400m), with more isolated buildings dotted all the way up to the crest of the ridge near the rocky heads of the Peñones, where the Albergue Universitario and the Parador Nacional de Sierra Nevada are situated. The 32-room Parador (3 stars) is open all year but is often full - book well in advance. Development of the complex is still ongoing.

Borreguiles is a small sub-centre situated higher up the valley head at 2650m. During periods of poor snow-cover, when the snowline is above Prado Llano, this tiny group of buildings becomes overcrowded as hundreds of skiers converge on it. Access to Borreguiles is either by ski-lift from the main centre, or (in summer) via a branch road from the Sierra Nevada Road (see road guide section).

WILD CAMPING

Camping is not officially permitted in the corrals of the high sierra, but tents are always in evidence during the summer months, so it is safe to assume that this rule is not enforced. Site your tent discreetly and you should have no trouble. Favourite sites for wild camping are the grassy shores of various tarns, such as those in the Cañada de las Siete Lagunas, Laguna de la Mosca (below Mulhacén's north face), and Laguna Larga (beneath the Crestones de Rio Seco). Slightly marred by the seemingly innate litter is the Cueva Secreta, in the upper Genil valley, but this is a popular and convenient campsite.

MOUNTAIN HUTS AND REFUGES

In years gone by, the Sierra Nevada was liberally provided with well appointed huts and refuges. Unfortunately, their proprietors have now largely abandoned the majority of them. With only one exception, all the huts of the high sector are now useful only as emergency shelters, and some are not even fit for that. It remains a mystery as to why such a large network of 'refugios' has been allowed to fall into ruin, particularly when the Sierra is experiencing something of a renaissance with the development of 'Prado Llano' and the building of new access tracks. The forestry commission and the Junta de Andalucia have refurbished some of the low-lying huts, built some new ones, and apparently have plans for more, but they seem to reserve the use of these huts to a few selected clubs and organisations. Perhaps bitter experience has taught them to be wary of allowing access to all and sundry?

Below is a list of the huts (west to east) which lie close to the routes described in this guide, along with their grid references and a note about their condition in 1993.

The Caballo bivouac hut. (Routes 27 and 33)

Refugio de Ventura - GR.588932
At the top edge of the forest by the path descending from Cerro del Caballo. In ruins.

Refugio de Lanjarón - GR.609959
Below Hoya del Zorro to the south of Caballo, near main path. Utterly ruined.

Refugio del Caballo - GR.612968
On the shore of Laguna del Caballo. A small bivouac hut. No more than a stone building with a fireplace. The hut is in good condition, but a little damp and smelly.

Refugio de Peñon Colorado - GR.637988
Below the Vereda Cortada path near the head of the Lanjarón valley. A semi-natural bivouac shelter. Quite roomy, but falling into disrepair.

Refugio de Lagunillos - GR.649994
On crest of Tajos de los Machos ridge above Laguna de Lanjarón. Razed to the ground.

Refugio de Elorrieta - GR.652997
On crest of main ridge at head of Lanjarón valley. Once a roomy and

well equipped hut. Now abandoned and crumbling. Built partly underground so still usable as a bivouac shelter.

Refugio de las Yeguas - GR.662015

At north end of Laguna de las Yeguas. Accessible by 4WD track. A new hut, so building is in good condition, but used as a toilet and rubbish dump by visitors. Not recommended.

Refugio del Cilindro - GR.670005

By the roadside at the Collado del Carijuela (Veleta col). A small cylindrical stone-built bivouac shelter. Abused in the same way as Las Yeguas hut. Incredibly squalid.

Refugio del Vadillo - GR.685094

On the south bank of the Rio Genil near confluence with Rio Vadillo. A small stone bivvie shelter similar to Caballo hut. In good condition.

Refugio de Felix Mendez - GR.694008

Situated in the Rio Seco corral, near to the South Sierra Nevada Road. The only large hut in the high Sierra which is in good repair. Warden in attendance in summer. Open to FEM and affiliated organisations. Small bivvie room left open during closed months. 50 beds, meals service, radio telephone. A very popular hut. Camping permitted in surrounding area.

Choza del Tio Papeles - GR.706077

On the Cuesta del Calvario above the Genil valley. Completely in ruins, but replaced by the **Refugio Forestal del Calvario** nearby. The new forestry hut is open only to organisations approved by the forestry commission.

Refugio Cueva Secreta - GR.707054

In the lower Valdeinfiernos valley at the foot of Loma de Casillas. Little more than a small wall and an overhanging boulder. Very popular with winter climbers heading for the north faces, as witnessed by the amount of litter.

Refugio Natural de Siete Lagunas - GR.738006

Above the Laguna Hondera in the Lower Cañada de las Siete Lagunas. Another natural bivvie shelter consisting of a wall built around a large overhanging outcrop. Useful in an emergency.

USING THE GUIDE

One of the difficulties faced by guidebook authors is attempting to grade routes, and estimate time allowances. I have decided to avoid this problem by generally not giving times or grades for the routes. The only exceptions are in cases where the walking is so easy that most people will make similar progress, and when discussing climbing routes. In the former case, an approximate time is mentioned in the route description, and in the latter case the official climbing grade is mentioned. However, I have given figures for each route in the form of the total distance in kilometres (measured from the 1:25,000 scale map with a cartographer's wheel), and the total amount of ascent in metres (measured by counting of contours on the same map). Most walkers will be able to estimate their times, taking account of the route description, their own level of fitness, the weather and the altitude and level of acclimatisation to it. All these factors have a pronounced influence on times. Do not underestimate the effect of altitude on the high routes, or the summer heat on the lower ones; both can reduce the fittest of walkers to a snail's pace.

Many of the routes can be linked together to form a longer outing, or sections of some routes can be used as an approach to another.

Where this is likely to interest the reader, mention is made in the text. The guide is intended to be used in conjunction with the local IGN mapping (see Maps and Guides below), and inventive readers will no doubt devise their own itineraries using the maps and the guide together.

Unless stated otherwise in the text, route descriptions assume summer conditions. That is, only isolated patches of snow, high temperatures, clear visibility and light winds. In bad weather, or winter conditions, the route will obviously be more serious, and will take proportionately longer to accomplish. In cases where winter conditions substantially alter the character of a route, the text discusses the respective pros and cons.

MOUNTAIN BIKING

The Sierra Nevada is networked with dirt tracks, and many of the paths - being dry and hard - lend themselves ideally to mountain biking. The area in general is a veritable playground for the adventurous cyclist, and the activity is very popular locally. Even for the walker, a suitable bike can take the toil out of what would be a long approach walk.

There are many mountain bike hire businesses in the area, and a local mountain bike route-guide (see Bibliography).

Because some of the walking routes are wholly or partly 'mountain bike friendly', I have included some comments, and a MBF appellation where this applies. However, the lack of a MBF label does not necessarily rule out a route to the all-terrain cyclist. It depends on the individual's skill, courage, and determination. Those marked MBF can be regarded as relatively 'rideable'.

FOUR-WHEEL-DRIVE VEHICLES (4WDs)

The internal road network consists largely of rough dirt roads, many of which are quite drivable in ordinary saloons, but some of which require the use of a 4WD. In this instance 4WD means a Land-Rover type vehicle, known as a 'todo terreno' (all terrain) locally, as opposed to a four-wheel-drive saloon, which would not have the necessary ground clearance. The road guide gives details of the nature of these tracks.

MAPS AND OTHER GUIDES

At the time of writing, there is only one other English guide to the Sierra Nevada, Robin Collomb's *Gredos Mountains and Sierra Nevada*, which is largely devoted to the Gredos near Madrid, and which contains only 24 pages of information on the Sierra Nevada. In Spanish, the choice is obviously wider, with at least two fairly comprehensive walkers' guidebooks, a mountain bikers' guide, and a large coffee-table book covering walking, skiing, and climbing in the Sierra. More details in the Bibliography.

Maps at 1:25,000 scale can be obtained from the Instituto Geográfico Nacional (IGN), and military maps at 1:50,000 from the Servicio Geográfico del Ejército (SGE). Besides these, the Federacion

Española de Montañismo (FEM) produces a huge sheet at 1:50,000 scale covering the entire area of this guide, which also has valuable information on hotels, with the ski facilities printed on the reverse. All these maps are useful, each carrying a certain amount of information which is unique to itself, but there are disagreements between them, too, some of the differences being quite major.

For planning a holiday in the Sierra, the FEM map is pre-eminent. Spread out on the floor, or a large table, the shading of this map gives a good impression of the range. However, many of the roads and paths are incorrectly marked on this map and for detailed planning, the more accurate IGN maps are recommended.

NOTE: Readers will notice on the IGN maps a number of features marked as 'Cañada Real'. These are shown as broad tracks or pathways, often marching straight across impossible terrain. They do not exist on the ground, and merely indicate the existence of a right of way under ancient bylaws for farmers to herd animals from one place to another.

For the purpose of this guide, I have adhered to altitudes quoted on the IGN maps, but with regard to place names, I have used the names and spellings accepted locally. In places, these do not agree with the IGN maps, but labelling on all the maps mentioned above leaves a lot to be desired - they are some way below Ordnance Survey standards. The addresses of map suppliers are given in the Bibliography.

EMERGENCY SERVICES

To all intents and purposes, there is no mountain rescue as a British mountaineer understands it in the Sierra Nevada during the summer months. In emergencies, your first contact should be the Guardia Civil who will organise rescue if necessary. It is worth remembering the radio telephone which exists at the Felix Mendez hut.

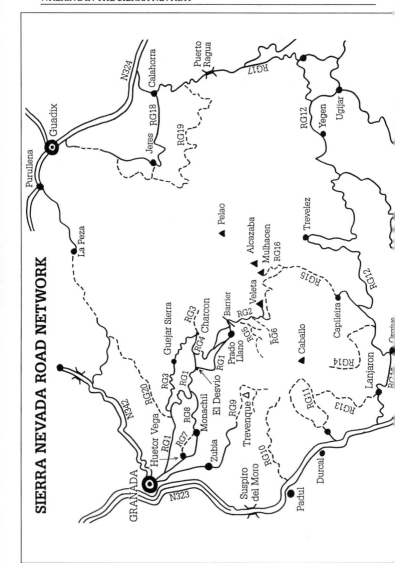

Road access within the Range

INTRODUCTION

The area of the guide is circumnavigated by a rough rectangle of roads. Travelling anti-clockwise from Granada, these are the N323 over Suspiro del Moro, the C333/GR421/C332/C331 Alpujarras and Puerto de la Ragua roads, the N324 to Guadix, and the N342 back to Granada. The main N roads require no description, but within this area many of the roads are rough or unsurfaced, and afford the only convenient approach to the peaks. The roads within the guide area are described below, numbered RG1 to RG20 (RG = Road Guide) and are divided into three grades: Easy, 4WD Recommended and 4WD Only. Tarmac roads and moderate dirt tracks are rated Easy. Most of my explorations were done in an ordinary Audi 80, but where deep ruts, or steep, loose gradients were encountered I have designated the route 4WD Recommended. Routes which demand the ground clearance and traction of a Land-Rover type vehicle are graded 4WD Only. Where a route is on the borderline, a double grading is given. All gradings assume dry summer conditions. In wet weather, or under snow, anything not graded Easy will require a 4WD vehicle, and many of the more difficult tracks may become impassable.

4WDs can be hired locally, at Bubión for instance, and also on the Costa del Sol, but charges are high - at least double the rate for a SEAT Marbella, which is itself a surprisingly useful 'off-roader'.

The 20 numbered Road Guides below do not represent an exhaustive list. The locals are prolific track-makers, and the whole area is criss-crossed with them (mountain bikers take note), but I have covered all the drivable ones which make useful approach routes. All the dirt tracks are ideal for mountain biking, most of them being very quiet with relatively easy gradients.

Descriptions follow, beginning in Granada, and progressing around the range in an anti-clockwise direction via Suspiro del

Moro, the Alpujarras, Puerto de la Ragua, Guadix, and back to Granada.

RG1. LOWER SIERRA NEVADA ROAD (GR420)
(To Parador Nacional)

EASY

The 'Carretera de Sierra Nevada' leaves the city along the north bank of the Rio Genil, passing through the straggling villages of Lancha de Cenes and Cenes de la Vega. The road remains level until the Genil is crossed at k 8, then begins climbing through scrubby terrain. This section has many bends as it gains 350m in 5km, passing turnings to Canales on the left at k 13.5, and El Purche on the right at k 16.5 and k 18.5. Just beyond k 22 there is a petrol station (the only one on the road) and the Hotel Santa Cruz with a superb view of Güéjar Sierra below. It is worth noting that up to this point there are a number of good, reasonably priced hotels along the roadside, with El Nogal, and El Desvio being worth a visit.

NOTE: During 1993 extensive work was underway to rebuild and improve this section of the road in preparation for the 1996 World Ski Championships.

At k 23 the road sweeps around a long hairpin bend (El Desvio) with another road branching straight on; this is the beginning of the comparatively new El Dornajo variation. This section was only completed in 1979 after considerable difficulties and expense had been encountered. The new 10km section actually cost more to build than the whole of the original road from Granada to Veleta. The old road (straight on at El Desvio bend) is now very quiet but is beginning to crumble in places. It rejoins the new road at the Sabinas col, above Prado Llano. This is the road marked on the SGE map.

The new road above El Desvio is superb. Broad and smooth, it climbs in long curves towards the stark-looking buildings of Prado Llano, which come into view after a rock gateway at k 26.5. Veleta still looks unimpressive from this point, but it is further away than it appears, and some 1500m higher.

At k 31 the turning into the ski centre is reached, the main road sweeping left to traverse back to the Sabinas col, where the original road is rejoined at the old k 31. The road through the ski centre can be followed as it climbs in zig-zags among the hotels to rejoin the main highway just before k 34.

Continuing on the main route from the ski centre entrance, the road doubles back in a north-westerly direction through pleasant pine woods, to join the old road at the aforementioned Collado de las Sabinas. From here, the surface deteriorates, becoming more pock-marked and lumpy, and cars begin to feel more underpowered and to produce more smoke as the altitude begins to be felt. The terrain is now more barren, the road climbing above the ski complex along the flank of the Peñones de San Francisco ridge (Veleta's North West Ridge). At k 35 (2475m above sea level) the Parador de Sierra Nevada is reached. The Parador occupies a commanding site, overlooking the huge basin of the upper Monachil valley, which houses almost the entire ski area. A dreary view in summer, but transformed into a dazzling and colourful scene when the slopes are snow-covered.

The road now makes a loop behind and above the Parador to gain the crest of the ridge at c.2500m by the distinctive military hostel called the Albergue de la Hoya de la Mora (always closed and shuttered). This is a popular stopping place, with plenty of parking space at each side of the road, and the Albergue Universitario nearby. A barrier closes the road from this point onwards during winter, and crowds of 'Granadinos' bring their children here for sledging on snowy weekends (sledges/skis etc. for hire at numerous roadside kiosks).

Prominent landmarks hereabouts are the observatory on the summit of the conical outcrop called 'El Mojón del Trigo' (literally The Cairn of Wheat), and the statue of the 'Virgen de las Nieves' (Virgin of the Snows).

Alcazaba from Veleta. Photo by Ian Roberts

RG2. UPPER SIERRA NEVADA ROAD (GR420)
(To Veleta summit)

EASY (during summer)

This, the highest road in Europe, is usually open from mid June to mid September, though it may be opened or closed sooner or later depending on prevailing conditions. In good weather it is an easy drive, and the summit roadhead is often crowded with tourists and hire cars from the Costa del Sol.

From the barrier at the Albergues (k 36), the road wends its way between the Mojón del Trigo and the Virgen de las Nieves, climbing in short loops at an easy gradient, though now quite narrow. Just before k 38 the wide turning to Borreguiles is passed on the right (see RG5) and the road begins to zig-zag more frequently, gaining height surprisingly quickly despite its easy angles. The hot air wafting through the windows at valley level has now given way to a wonderfully fresh breeze.

As the 2900m level is passed, vegetation on the roadsides gives way to the barren, bouldery terrain of 'alta montaña', and fallen stones often litter the road. On a left-hand hairpin bend the 'Altitud 3050m' sign is passed and on the next left hairpin is the turning onto the unmade road to the Yeguas hut (see RG6).

After one more zig-zag, the road reaches the crest of Veleta's main north ridge (c.3100m small ruined buildings on left at right-hand bend). Small parking spaces on left and right allow access to the edge of crags (Tajos del Veleta), from where there are superb views of the mountain's impressive Pared Norte (North Wall). The path into the Corral del Veleta via the Veredon Superior (Route 23) also commences here.

Having gained the ridge, the road promptly leaves it in favour of a long climbing traverse across the western slopes (much used as an 'inter-pista' link by skiers in winter). At the 3200m contour the road forks, and there is an area wide enough for the buses from Granada to turn round - this is as far as you go by bus! From this point, a direct ascent over boulders may be made to reach the ridge crest near the summit.

The right fork descends slightly to a notch in the main crest of the range (Collado del Veleta), where the tarmac ends and whence the Southern Sierra Nevada Road continues as a dirt track (RG15). The left fork leads via numerous zig-zags to an abrupt dead end just a few metres from the summit of Veleta, where there are usually a couple of very expensive souvenir/snack stalls. There is little room to turn around at the roadhead and it is a good idea to stop before reaching the end, where the verges are wider.

RG3. GÜÉJAR SIERRA AND GENIL VALLEY ROAD (GR460)
(To San Juan)

EASY

At k 8 on the Sierra Nevada Road (just prior to crossing the river) the road branches left and climbs quickly in sweeping bends to the top of the dam at the end of the Embalse de Canales. From the dam there is a good view of the rock stack known as the Pulpito de Canales, at the foot of which the village of the same name stood before the building of the reservoir in 1985. The terraces on which the houses were built are still visible. The bar at the Las Lomas campsite has an old picture of the village and the Pulpito on the wall.

Continuing above the reservoir the road becomes narrower, passing the Las Lomas campsite before entering the village of Güéjar Sierra. As the road approaches the village centre, a right fork (signposted 'Charcon Maitena' and 'Sierra Nevada') leads to a rough, makeshift 'bypass' around the south side of the pueblo, leading via a steep climb to a T-junction, where a right turn brings you onto the Genil valley road. This road is narrow, crumbly, and occasionally precipitous as it plunges down to the bed of the valley. Along this stretch, a number of junctions on the left promise access to the valley of the Rio Maitena, but these are too rough to be recommended to drivers of non-4WD cars.

At the valley bed, the road joins the line of the Tranvia de Sierra Nevada, a tramway which once carried trippers from Granada up the Genil to the terminus (Estacion de San Juan) at 1150m. Opened in 1925, the tranvia or ferrocarril (railway) was a remarkable feat of engineering, entailing the construction of a number of tunnels and some extremely elegant bridges. Unfortunately, it never achieved the popularity it deserved, partly because of the construction of the Sierra Nevada Road in the 1930s. Nevertheless, the Tranvia continued to operate until 1974, finally being killed off by the projected Embalse de Canales. Until recently, one of the old trams could still be seen in the park by the Paseo de la Bomba in Granada (beginning of Sierra Nevada Road), and the station buildings are still standing at Pinos Genil, Maitena, Charcon, and San Juan.

From the confluence of the rios Genil and Maitena, where the road from Güéjar Sierra arrives at the valley bottom, the line of the tramway makes a convenient track up the valley. Although narrow and unsurfaced, the track is easy and not many cars are met except on Sundays when it is best avoided. After passing through 2 of 5 tunnels and just before entering the third, a junction will be seen on the right with a new bridge carrying the road over onto the south bank (see RG4). Continuing through the third tunnel, the Charcon bar and the station ruin will be seen across the river, and the old platform on the left. This is a popular picnic spot with local people during the summer holidays.

The track continues through tunnel 4, passing private open-air swimming pools and another bar (sometimes closed) before crossing

Merendero de la Fuente del Hervidero with Trevenque and Cuerda del Trevenque behind *(Photo by Glyn Denver)*
Cortijo Sevilla col and Los Alayos de Dilar *(Photo by Glyn Denver)*

a high bridge with the bar Chiquito opposite. This bar is recommended, despite its ramshackle appearance, for its atmosphere, cuisine, and low prices. The terrace overlooks a popular bathing pool under the bridge with a rope swing.

Beyond Chiquito, the track passes the start of the Vereda de la Estrella (just before re-crossing the river and entering tunnel 5) but this is not the normal place to join the Vereda - most people continue to the roadhead and join it there. Emerging from tunnel 5, a traverse above the north bank of the river soon brings you to the roadhead at the foot of the Barranco de San Juan with its small parking area (often full on Sundays) adjacent to the former Estacion de San Juan.

RG4. GENIL VALLEY TO SIERRA NEVADA LINK ROAD
(Charcon - El Desvio)

EASY

This road affords a simple route from the Upper Genil to the Sierra Nevada Old Road near El Desvio, and thus to the ski-resort. Commencing at Charcon (see above) the road climbs quite steeply in crumbly zig-zags to the Hotel del Duque (deeply shrouded in trees, and mystery), and then improves as it loops around and above the 'hotel'. A road leading off left leads only to private farms in the San Juan 'barranco'.

The surface improves steadily, though the road is still narrow, and as more open terrain is reached so the views open up spectacularly. Güéjar Sierra is especially well seen from here, and looking back yields a vista of the surprisingly close-looking 3000m ridge. The architecture of the upper barrancos leading up into the north face zone is well appreciated from this viewpoint.

Presently, the road reaches a T-junction with the Sierra Nevada Old Road. A right turn leads to El Desvio in 200m, while turning left will lead you (via the old road) to the Collado de las Sabinas, above Prado Llano.

Approaching Pico de la Carne via the south-west ridge. (Route 2)

RG5. BORREGUILES ACCESS ROAD (from Upper Sierra Nevada (Veleta) Road)

EASY
Almost at k 38 on the main Veleta road, a wide and obvious road leads off rightwards, descending gradually into the basin of the Monachil valley-head. The road is badly surfaced, but completely straightforward, and leads directly to the tiny cluster of buildings at Borreguiles which forms a sort of subsidiary ski station.

NOTE: The continuation of this road carries many dire warning signs ('Carretera Cortada' - road cut, and 'Muy Peligroso' - very dangerous, etc), but your intrepid author has ascertained that the road is in fact easy and leads to the radio telescope which is a prominent landmark on the slopes of Veleta. There is plenty of parking space near the telescope and no-one has objected when I have parked there. This is a possible alternative starting point for the approach to the Yeguas hut, and thence to the Elorietta hut.

RG6. YEGUAS HUT ACCESS TRACK (from Upper Sierra Nevada (Veleta) Road)

4WD RECOMMENDED
This track departs from the Veleta road above the 3050m contour (see RG2 for location). An additional landmark is a 'Competicion Pista' starting hut on the slopes above the junction. The track is rough, and has been compromised by rockfalls in places. The final zig-zags down to the hut are very rocky and only cars with good ground clearance will negotiate them without worrying clonks emanating from beneath. It is probably fair to say that most small family cars will manage it, but it is really only recommended for 4WD vehicles. Continuation roads leading off in the direction of the observatory and Borreguiles are definitely only for 4WDs.

RG7. CAMINO DE LOS NEVEROS (Huetor Vega - El Purche)

4WD RECOMMENDED

This completely unmade track is the old route by which ice and snow was brought down from the mountains during winter, hence the name (loosely Route of the Snows). It commences at the small sub-development of Huetor Vega called Los Rebites, and climbs along the low ridge bounding the southern side of the Genil valley, with good views of the villages therein, before joining the tarmac service road from Monachil just before reaching El Purche.

As a route for cars, the camino has little to recommend it, being rough, occasionally steep, and in the latter stages very narrow. Passable in cars with good ground clearance/determined drivers, easy in a 4WD, absolutely ideal on a mountain bike.

Leaving Granada via the Paseo de la Bomba, as if heading for the Sierra Nevada Road, turn right at the first bridge over the Genil (Puente Verde), and immediately bear left, slightly uphill, into the Avenida de Cervantes. At the top of the hill the road passes the last shops on the right and emerges into more open country. Take the next left turning in 200m, heading steeply uphill via a big double bend to enter Los Rebites amid unfortunate unofficial rubbish dumps. Follow the road through the estate until the tarmac ends, with the popular Bar Perdices dead ahead, and then turn right up a gradual dusty incline. This is the start of the Camino de los Neveros.

After winding its way through more unsightly rubbish, the track eventually climbs clear of the dumps and begins to curl around and between various low, sandy hills (very popular with the local motorbike scramblers). After a couple of rough and loose ascents, the Camino traverses along the northern slopes of the 1360m Majojos, overlooking the villages in the Genil valley - not for nervous drivers!

After negotiating a slight hummock, the track joins the relatively new service road ascending from Monachil (see RG8 below).

RG8. MONACHIL SERVICE ROAD
(Monachil - Sierra Nevada via El Purche)

EASY

This excellent tarmac road was built to allow easy access for service vehicles to the Sierra Nevada ski-resort, which lies within the municipal responsibility of the village of Monachil, which is probably smaller than the ski-resort itself.

Access to the road through the village is tortuous and not at all obvious - if the wrong bridge over the rio is used, you will fall foul of the infamous 'maniobra', an extremely narrow and acute 'Z' between buildings which entails driving forward along the first straight, reversing back up the diagonal, and then driving out. It is practically impossible to drive through the 'maniobra' (manoeuvre) conventionally; diagramatic signposts give directions.

Entering the village from the direction of Granada and Huetor Vega, take the second bridge on the left, crossing the river and then turning right to skirt the north side of the village via a typically narrow Andalucian village street. Turning left at the next T-junction will bring you up out of the village on a steep, narrow lane with steps in the middle for mules(!). All this looks very unlikely, but eventually emerges onto the much wider tarmac of the service road. Adjacent to the road at this point is an old threshing platform, now used as a parking area by climbers and walkers visiting Los Cahorros. The path to the gorge is signposted just below the parking area.

From this point the road is good, though lacking barriers, and zig-zags rapidly up to the crest of the Pueblo-Majojos ridge, where the Camino de los Neveros joins on the left. The road soon passes the bar at El Purche and crosses a tract of open country before descending through sparse pines to the Sierra Nevada Road between k 18 and k 19. At El Purche, a steeper unmade road branches left to descend to the main road between k 16 and k 17, but this has little advantage over the much smoother tarmac road.

RG9. HUENES VALLEY FORESTRY ROAD
(La Zubia to Huenes/Dilar valleys)

EASY

This excellent road is a popular local excursion and provides the only vehicular approach to the Cumbres Verdes (Green Summits) region which contains all the 'peaches' of Baja Montaña.

Commencing on the south-eastern edge of the village of La Zubia (signposted 'Cumbres Verdes' and 'La Guitarra bar') the road climbs relentlessly through rather scruffy picnic areas among the Pinares de la Zubia, gaining 500m in under 2 miles, to reach the desirable residences of the Cumbres Verdes development, centred on the La Guitarra bar and restaurant. Here the good tarmac gives way to a crumbling, neglected version which demands constant meandering to avoid profound ruts and potholes.

After passing through a plantation, the road climbs along open slopes, passing the Merendero de la Fuente del Hervidero (busy on Sundays) before looping eastwards towards the imposing peak of Trevenque and the entrance to the narrow defile of the Huenes valley. The peak rising on the right on this section is Boca de la Pesca, while across the valley on the left rises the sparsely wooded mass of Huenes with its subsidiaries Cerro del Tamboril and Pico de la Carne. Presently, the road begins a gentle descent, at the top of which it passes a side turning on the right, going uphill to a parking area. Roughly painted signs on boulders here proclaim 'Finca Privado, Prohibido el Paso' (private farm, passage prohibited), but no-one seems to object to parking at this point.

This is the Cortijo Sevilla col (farm ruins below, new holiday homes nearby), affording a superb view across the Dilar valley to the serrated ridge of Los Alayos de Dilar. Many walks start from here.

Back on the main route, the track now throws off all pretence of tarmac respectability, and is a lot better for it. The broad gravel forest road descends gently to enter the ravine of the Huenes valley. A new development during 1993 was the addition of a chain barrier ('cadena') on this stretch. The barrier is usually open but can be used as a means of controlling access to the forest during times of high

Cortijo Sevilla col and Los Alayos de Dilar

fire-risk.

The road now climbs up on a terrible washboard surface to cross the Puente de los Siete Ojos (Bridge of the Seven Eyes), where parking can be found for the start of the Pico de la Carne path. Continuing on the true right bank of the normally dry river, the track climbs gradually, giving excellent views of Trevenque as it winds its way through sparse woodland. As the head of the valley is approached, the road arrives at the Casa Forestal de la Cortijuela. This is a delectable spot, with a pleasant grassy bank, drinking 'fuente', shady trees and a band of crag overlooking the scene. From here, paths go off in various directions to reach the Cerro Gordo/Pico del Tesoro/Cerro del Mirador ridge, which overlooks the Monachil valley.

The large fenced enclosure on the south side of the road at this point is the botanical garden, which is planted with an example of each of the species of flora to be found in the Sierra Nevada. Anyone interested in the rich botany of the area can obtain permission to look around the Jardin Botanico. Contact ICONA (national conservation institute) at Gran Via de San Francisco 35, 28079, MADRID, or ask at the Casa Cortijuela if occupied.

The track now loops around to the south, skirting Trevenque's shattered eastern slopes, crosses the Collado de Martin (or Trevenque), and descends towards the Rio Dilar. At two small farm buildings (a goat-trading post) adjacent to the Collado de Chaquetas, the road forks. The left fork descends with difficulty (not recommended) to a dead end among old quarry workings, and still some distance from the valley bed. The right fork crosses the col and then encounters a locked chain barrier with a no entry sign. On foot, or on mountain bike, the continuation can be followed as it descends via a new refugio (locked) and the derelict Casa Rosales towards the Dilar bed and Toma del Canal. During the summer of 1992, a bulldozer extended this road beyond the river bed and some distance downstream of Toma del Canal with the apparent intention of making a link with either Cortijo Sevilla or the village of Dilar itself. The road remained a dead end throughout 1993 however.

Close to the river bed, this track crosses the path from Cortijo Sevilla to Toma del Canal. Thus, mountain bikers can make a circuit of Trevenque starting and finishing at Cortijo Sevilla, a fine expedition with superb scenery throughout.

RG10. ERMITA VIEJA/LOS MIRADORES ROAD
(from Aguadero)

4WD RECOMMENDED

The steep, wooded slopes and quarries above the main road (N323) near Padul seem impregnable, but a narrow dirt track snakes its way up, climbing along the southern slopes of the Silleta del Padul. This track penetrates a considerable distance into the complex steep-sided tributary barrancos of the upper Durcal valley (eventual link with Torrente system possible for two-wheeled vehicles), but becomes progressively more difficult after crossing the large saddle known as Los Miradores. With care, a 2WD saloon with good ground clearance will get as far as Los Miradores in good conditions, but beyond there the route is best left to 4WD vehicles.

Los Miradores is a convenient starting point for the ascent of Picacho Alto, at the western end of the Los Alayos ridge, and also provides access to the southern side of the upper Dilar valley.

The start of the Los Miradores track is not obvious. Coming from Granada on the main N323 road, the turning is just beyond k 153 (near Restorante Montesol on the right). The main road sweeps left and right at this point, and the turning is just after the left-hand bend. Initially follow the broad quarry access road (follow Aridos Padul and Ermitas Viejas sign), climbing quite steeply towards the quarry entrance, but 500m from the main road look for a small dirt track on the right (partly obscured by trees), signposted 'Ermitas Viejas'. This is the track to Los Miradores.

The lower part of this track is often messed about by the quarry. The route through the quarry varies in difficulty from year to year, but it is always kept open. The track soon climbs clear of the workings and begins threading its way up the wooded flank of La Silleta. The track is very narrow, occasionally rough, and traverses above some awesome drops with only a line of flimsy pine trees to protect the edge. Hairpin bends are numerous, a couple of them being very acute - a Fiat Panda 4x4 or Suzuki SJ would be preferable to a Range Rover for this route.

After wending its way upward for a considerable distance, the track levels out near the broad crest of Cerro Domingo (1475m) and enters more open country. Two forks are encountered. Keep right at both, the second branch leading leftwards down to the Casa Sierra and Ermita Vieja - a farm and old hermitage, where there is a 'pozo' or well. An attractive new hut, designed to look old, but with solar roof panels, has been built near to the well. Four-wheel drive recommended for the descent to this hut.

The main route continues on a good sandy surface for a while as it skirts the head of the Barranco del Puerto before rising to a sharp hairpin bend on the crest of a subsidiary ridge linking Cerro de Montellano (1404m) and Cerro de Loma Alta (1532m).

This latter hill is marked on the IGN (Padul) map, with Los Miradores nearby, but is given the name 'Los Miradores' on the SGE (Padul) map. Probably, the 'miradores' (viewpoints) are to be found all around this area, but the large tree-less saddle to the east of Cerro Montellano is the place usually given this name locally.

From the acute bend at the ridge crest, the track descends roughly on loose stones with some deep ruts to reach the large flat clearing on the Los Miradores saddle. Parking here is no problem, but it may be wise in summer to leave your car in the shade on the fringes of the clearing to avoid returning to the vehicle to find all the controls too hot to touch!

On the eastern edge of the clearing, a good path to Picacho Alto and Los Alayos commences.

The track gets progressively rougher from here, and leads into the Durcal valley. The link with the Torrente track network (impassable to four-wheeled vehicles) is possible on a trials bike or mountain bike, thus opening up the possibility of a long dirt road traverse from Padul to Lanjarón via Los Miradores, Torrente and Caballo south-west ridge tracks.

RG11. ARROYO DE TORRENTE TRACK SYSTEM

4WD ONLY

Driving south from Granada along the N323, the Rio Torrente is the next river to be crossed after the Rio Durcal. Unlike the Dilar and Durcal valleys, which are long, narrow and enclosed, the Torrente is a vast 'cwm' encompassing many tributaries, and is encircled by high ridges falling from the summit of Cerro del Caballo (3013m) - the most westerly of the Sierra Nevada 3000-ers. The enclosing ridges are called the Loma de los Tres Mojones (Ridge of the Three Cairns), and Loma de las Tres Encinas (encina' = holm-oak tree).

The slopes of this huge cirque are criss-crossed by a number of dirt tracks, all accessed via the delectable little village of Nigüelas. Many of these track are easy, but some are in a bad state, and would even give a Land-Rover considerable difficulty. With determination, it is possible to reach a height of 2150m below Caballo, but the Torrente valley is generally unattractive, and better approaches to this 'final' 3000-er are to be found on the Lanjarón side of the mountain.

There is a possible link with the Durcal valley, and thence with the Los Miradores track from this track system, but one short section is only passable to trials or enduro motorcyclists, or mountain bikers.

RG12. LANJARÓN TO LAROLES VIA LAS ALPUJARRAS
(C333/GR421)

EASY

This tarmac road serves as the southern boundary of the area covered by this guide, traversing the lower slopes of the Sierra Nevada, and passing through the villages of the upper Alpujarras. Unmade roads branch off northward at various points to penetrate the southern valleys, and at Pampaneira commences the South Sierra Nevada Road, which ascends to join the tarmac of the Sierra Nevada Road near Veleta summit, thus providing a link over the main ridge to Granada. However, this is not a short cut. It takes much longer to go from Pampaneira to Granada via the Sierra Nevada Road than via Lanjarón and Suspiro del Moro.

The Alpujarras road starts near the remarkable cutting at Tablate bridge on the N323. Immediately after passing through the cutting coming from Granada, the turning is on the left signposted Lanjarón (40min/40km from Granada).

The C333 is quite narrow and tortuous, and the entire route follows this pattern. Average speeds are very low, and some suggested time allowances from Granada are included in the description below to provide some guidance to readers.

Lanjarón, a large spa town famous for its Agua de la Sierra Nevada mineral water, is 7km along the road (50min from Granada) and its attractive, shady main street is narrow and often clogged with pedestrians and haphazardly parked vehicles. The C333 continues to the capital of the western Alpujarra, Orgiva, but before reaching this large village a turning on the left (just beyond k 16) brings you onto the GR421, which climbs up to traverse the slopes above, giving good views over Orgiva. After passing turnings to Cañar, and Soportujar, the white buildings of the Ermita del Padre Eterno appear on the right. Directly opposite is the beginning of the Chico/Lanjarón valley track (RG14). In a further 5km the road turns into the mouth of the striking Poquiera ravine, with the moorish villages of Capileira, Bubión, and Pampaneira clinging improbably to the steep eastern slopes.

The road loops down and crosses the ravine near the Pampaneira hydro-electrical works, before climbing in zig-zags through the village to the junction with the South Sierra Nevada Road (GR411), which is marred by a huge and disgusting rubbish dump on the roadside - a smelly place! The GR411 provides access to Bubión and Capileira. This point is about 1hr 40min from Granada (72km).

Moving swiftly on, the road traverses steep slopes giving breathtaking views of the lower Alpujarras, passing through Pitres (where there is a good campsite) and Portugos before descending slightly to Busquistar. All these villages have the characteristic appearance of Alpujarran 'pueblos', with white flat-roofed houses and a square-towered church.

After passing Busquistar, the GR421 turns north into the long narrow Trevélez valley. The road can be seen across the valley as it returns along the opposite slopes after visiting the village. Climbing steadily, the road eventually reaches the highest village in Spain at 1480m (2hr 10min/90km). Actually, Trevélez (as its name suggests) consists of three villages, or 'barrios', built one above the other with the highest buildings near to the 1600m contour, but the road only passes through the lower of the three. Trevélez has an excellent campsite, and provides a good base for exploring the southern valleys of Mulhacén and Alcazaba.

After returning south down the east side of the valley, the road turns eastward again, and immediately enters gentler, more open country. After passing through the attractive Juviles, and by the less attractive Berchules and Alcútar, the GR421 reaches a T-junction with the C332 (2hr 45min/112km). Turn left here to pass through Mecina Bombarón and reach Yegen (3hr/122km) where Gerald Brenan, the English author of the classic *South from Granada* and *The Face of Spain*, lived between 1920 and 1934.

The road, happily, passes above the village, and cars can be left at a small parking area if the village is to be explored. Yegen cannot have changed much since Brenan's days here, although there are now three bars and a 'supermercado' (supermarket). Gerald Brenan's house (which has a commemorative plaque) is near the top of the village, just around the corner from the Bar Nueva de la Fuente.

Continuing, the road passes through Valor, which is even more attractive than Yegen in some ways, and soon reaches the left turning to Laroles which will be reached in about 3$^{1}/_{2}$ hours' driving from Granada (139km). At Laroles, keep left above the village to reach a T-junction with a signpost pointing left to La Calahorra. This is the way to the Puerto de la Ragua - the eastern boundary of the guide. See RG17 for a description of the Ragua Pass road.

RG13. CABALLO SOUTH RIDGE TRACK NETWORK

Mostly EASY

The long ridge descending roughly south from Cerro del Caballo to Lanjarón has seen considerable development of vehicular access during recent years, with new dirt tracks reaching as high as 2320m - higher than the Ventura hut ruins and quite close to Caballo's summit. Continuation of this highest track (incomplete in 1993) will possibly link up with the Torrente network, which in turn links up with the Los Miradores/Silleta del Padul road, providing a spectacular high level traverse for mountain bikers.

NOTE: the link between Torrente and Los Miradores is not passable to four-wheeled vehicles due to water erosion and landslips in the upper Durcal valley.

RG14. CHICO VALLEY AND LANJARÓN VALLEY ACCESS TRACK

EASY

Commencing at the Ermita del Padre Eterno (see RG12 above) this relatively smooth track climbs sinuously around the slopes of the Chico valley before crossing the Loma de Cañar and entering the Lanjarón valley. Quite easily drivable in ordinary saloon cars, this track penetrates a considerable distance into the middle Lanjarón before giving way to a path, which is non-motorable but ideal for mountain bikes. This path leads to the Elorrieta hut ruins on the crest of the main ridge at c.3150m at the head of the valley.

NOTE: the forestry commission plan to replace the old Refugio Forestal at the end of the track with a new and better equipped hut.

RG15. SOUTH SIERRA NEVADA ROAD (GR411)
Pampaneira to Veleta Col

EASY

The GR411 leaves the GR421 Alpujarras road (RG12 above) at the rather smelly rubbish dump junction near Pampaneira. Climbing up the eastern slopes of the striking Poqueira ravine the tarmac road visits the pretty, moorish villages of Bubión and Capileira, with their white walled, flat roofed houses seemingly piled one on top of another on the steep slopes. At Bubión, a certain amount of development is going on, with holiday homes and souvenir shops springing up. 4WDs can also be hired here. This is a possible precursor to similar developments of other upper Alpujarras villages. Perhaps 'the thin end of the wedge'?

Until September 1963, the road did not progress far beyond Capileira, but in that month work began on the dirt road which would eventually link up with the tarmac Sierra Nevada Road near the summit of Veleta. The work continued until July 1967, when the two roads were joined, providing a trans-Sierra Nevada 'highway'.

Above Capileira, the tarmac continues for a kilometre or so, before giving way to a rough and dusty track, which winds gradually up through patches of forest in long easy zig-zags. The surface here is dirt and small stones, not too rough on the suspension, and the gradients are easy, giving no traction difficulties. As the road climbs, the surface deteriorates, becoming more stony and rutted, demanding good ground clearance as the broad top of El Chorillo (2722m) is approached.

El Chorillo marks the road's arrival on the broad back of the Loma del Mulhacén, and there is a sudden view of the jagged main ridge in the distance, with the Rio Seco arêtes and Veleta on the left. An inclined parking area on the right gives a view of Trevélez below, a viewpoint which allows you to appreciate just how high Spain's highest village really is.

A few metres further, a junction is encountered with a normal roadsign announcing 'Mulhacén', a rather incongruous fixture on Iberia's highest mountain! This is the start of the Mulhacén Summit Road (see below).

The Felix Mendez hut and Raspones de Rio Seco from South Sierra Nevada Road

The main road now begins a long (5km), very gradual traversing climb along Mulhacén's west flank to the Laguna de la Caldera (3036m) beneath the crest of the main ridge. Near to the 'laguna' (tarn), flat areas allow ample parking space on the roadside, and this is a popular picnic site on summer weekends. The Mulhacén col is easily accessed from here, and the summit itself can be reached in under an hour via the west flank.

The road now becomes much more stony as it makes a long loop south around the end of the Loma Pelada, returning north to hug the side of the pinnacled ridge known as the Crestones de Rio Seco (Crests of Dry River). Below on the left is the Refugio de Felix Mendéz, occupying a low hummock on the floor of a broad cwm. A track wriggles down to the hut, but unauthorised vehicles are discouraged by a chain barrier (sometimes padlocked).

The road now passes through a notch blasted from the Raspones de Rio Seco ridge ('raspon' = a graze or scratchmark) and continues to traverse stonily, keeping close to the very crest of the main ridge. Gaps between gendarmes along here afford magnificent views into the Corral de Valdeinfierno.

When the ridge rises abruptly to the summit of Cerro de los Machos, the road veers left, cutting across huge scree slopes which threaten to engulf it at any moment, but which settle for carpeting it with a layer of boneshaking stones. Those with mechanical sympathy will cringe at the punishing vibration caused by this unforgiving surface. Continuing through a landscape of huge shattered boulders, the road passes below the aggressive summit prow of Veleta, before climbing up via two acute hairpin bends to the Collado del Veleta where the tarmac of the GR420 is mercifully met. The Refugio del Cilindro is located at the roadside at this point. It consists of a cylindrical stone building with a low entrance, and is so squalid that it is hard to envisage anyone spending the night there. Even in an emergency a snowhole would seem preferable.

There is a small parking area at the col and paths commence from here to Veleta (of course) and to the western end of the main ridge.

RG16. MULHACÉN SUMMIT ROAD

4WD RECOMMENDED
The Mulhacén road reaches to the very crest of the summit ridge, stopping only when within 800m of the top, adjacent to the south summit (3400m). It winds its way upward in a series of loops and zig-zags initially, and then resorts to five straightish climbing traverses on the broader slopes above 300m.

Gradients are easy throughout, giving no problems even for a low-powered car. However, the surface is very rough and stony, demanding fairly good ground clearance and a degree of disregard for the wellbeing of the vehicle. Although ordinary cars frequently make it to the top, a 4WD is definitely more suitable.

RG17. PUERTO DE LA RAGUA (Laroles to La Calahorra)

EASY
Forming the eastern boundary of the area covered, this pass offers a scenic and easy crossing of the main spine of the range. The

scenery is pleasantly wooded and surprisingly green even in August. If contemplating a complete circuit of the Sierra Nevada by car, commencing with the Alpujarra road (RG12 above), then the return to Granada from Laroles takes approximately 1hr 45min to 2 hours if the Autovia from Guadix is used. A sensible time for the whole circuit, allowing for stops, is about 6 to 7 hours.

The ascent of the Ragua pass from Laroles is easy, the road having been completely rebuilt during the late 1980s. Prior to this it was just another dirt track, but it is now comparable to the Sierra Nevada Road. The new road climbs initially in a series of long sweeping bends, before straightening out as it gains the easy angles of the upper Bayarcal valley. The turning to the village of Bayarcal is passed at the 1750m contour and the valley then becomes more enclosed as the summit of the 'puerto' is approached.

At the top (2000m) there is a 'fuente' (but the water is not nearly as good as that from the Yegen fuente), and a pleasant picnic area, with the unfortunate litter which attends all Spanish beauty spots. Relatively easy paths lead off on both sides of the road to the adjacent lower main ridge summits of Chullo (2609m) and Morron (2730m).

The descent to La Calahorra is a complete contrast to the ascent, with the road plunging down the northern slopes in a series of narrow and bumpy hairpin bends with dire warning notices. The views over the Marquesado forests and the plains of Guadix are breathtaking, with the picturesque four-towered castle on its hillock at La Calahorra appearing far below, like a sandcastle on a beach.

As height is lost, the scale of the castle is more readily appreciated, and just before reaching the valley, the road suddenly improves, doubling in width and becoming silky smooth. After the bumps of the descent, this suave surface seems to waft you down to La Calahorra on a cushion of air.

RG18. LA CALAHORRA TO GUADIX VIA JERÉS DEL MARQUESADO

EASY

From La Calahorra, the direct route to Guadix is via a straight, flat road north to the N324, but a more scenic alternative is to turn left (west) and meander along the minor road through Jerés del Marquesado and then turn northwards to reach the main road just outside Guadix. The final section of this road is still unsurfaced (1992) and has some vicious washboard sections, caused by lorries, but the section along the foot of the Marquesado del Zenete forest makes it well worthwhile.

RG19. MARQUESADO DEL ZENETE FOREST ROAD

4WD RECOMMENDED

This relatively smooth dirt track makes a scenic outing for mountain bikers or 4WD drivers. Commencing in the east near the summit of the Ragua Pass road, the track traverses across the northern slopes of the Sierra Nevada's lower eastern hills, passing through the superb Marquesado del Zenete forest. The track is circuitous, winding in and out of every valley in the interests of maintaining a fairly constant height. At the western end, the track reaches the Porterillo hut, and then descends fairly directly to Jerés del Marquesado.

RG20. PURULLENA AND LA PEZA ROAD
(short cut Guadix - Granada)

EASY

The building of the new Autovias in the vicinity of Granada, and to Guadix, has made this one-time shortcut less of an advantage. Previously, the route provided a quick way to go from Güéjar Sierra or Sierra Nevada (ski complex) to Guadix, without having to pass through Granada and the lorry-infested N342 over the Sierra Harana.

The building of the Autovias in 1991-1993 has slashed the travelling time from Granada to Guadix to about 45 minutes. However, this route is interesting and a lot less frenetic than mixing it with the hard-charging drivers on the Autovia.

On the Sierra Nevada Road out of Granada, after passing through Cenes de la Vega but before reaching the Güéjar Sierra turning, a road branches left (signposted to Dudar and Quéntar). This is the way to Purulena. The route is mostly on tarmac. There is a short stretch of unmade road beyond the Embalse de Quéntar but this soon joins a tarmac road which leads via Tocón and La Peza to Purulena on the old main road just outside Guadix.

PART TWO:
Baja Montaña (Low Mountains)

INTRODUCTION

Baja Montaña is the term usually applied to the area of lower summits bordering the valleys radiating from Veleta's north-west flanks, including the Cumbres Verdes region, and the Alayos de Dilar. All the tops in this area occur on ridges dividing the four valleys which drain this side of Veleta, carrying the rios Monachil, Dilar, Durcal, and Torrente. A tributary of the Monachil, the Arroyo del Huenes, provides access to the centre of a fine group of summits via a well graded forestry road (RG9), and most of the best walks start from this side-valley.

For exploration of Baja Montaña, Granada makes a convenient base, as does La Zubia. Other villages, such as Monachil, Dilar, Padul, Durcal, etc are not as well provided with accommodation, and have no other advantages.

The Arroyo del Huenes, by far the most scenic, and the most popular, region is often referred to as Cumbres Verdes (Green Summits). The area is easily reached from La Zubia (pron. thoo-bee-a) via the Huenes valley road (RG9), and contains the majestic limestone summit of Trevenque (2079m), without doubt the 'king peak' of Baja Montaña.

The other gem of Baja Montaña is Los Alayos de Dilar. This serrated ridge bounds the south side of the Dilar valley and contains a number of abrupt peaks over 1800m, the best known being the imposing double summit of Corazón de la Sandía. The ridge is well seen from the Cortijo Sevilla col, adjacent to the Huenes valley road, but it is not so easily accessed (see below).

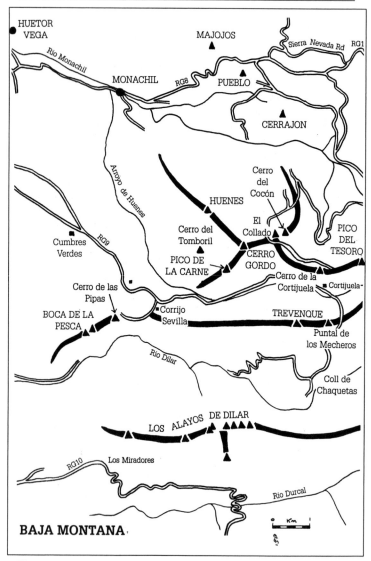

ROUTE 1. ASCENT OF BOCA DE LA PESCA FROM CORTIJO SEVILLA (on Huenes Valley road RG9)

Figures: 6km/180m 2hrs (including Cerro de las Pipas)

Boca de la Pesca ('Mouth of the Fish') takes its name from its resemblance to a fish-head when seen from the north-east, a view especially well seen from Cerro del Tamboril. It makes an ideal objective for an evening walk, little more than a stroll, offering good views over La Vega, and a fine panorama of the Cumbres Verdes.

From the parking area at Cortijo Sevilla, follow the obvious broad track heading south-west and west towards the little peak of Cerro de las Pipas. This eventually gives way to a choice of paths skirting the north-western slopes of the Pesca/Pipas ridge, which all converge at the foot of the 'fish-head' before climbing in two long zig-zags to emerge on the (lower) west summit where stands a curious domed shelter. There is a spectacular view down the plunging south face to the Dilar gorge with its hydro-electrical station, powered by the water from the Espartera canal.

The pointed peak of the higher east summit may be visited across the Boca in 5 minutes but descent is best made by the ascent route, which can be varied by following the ridge over Cerro de las Pipas (1426m).

ROUTE 2. ASCENT OF PICO DE LA CARNE FROM PUENTE DE LOS SIETE OJOS (on Huenes Valley Road RG9)

Figures: 3.5km/380m 1hr at most

Although it is really just a prominent outcrop on the edge of the Huenes massif, a prominent rocky summit and a steep narrow ridge make Carne well worth climbing for its own sake. At the Puente de los Siete Ojos, parking can be found either just before or just after the bridge, along the roadside. The path commences at the north-eastern end of the bridge, climbing diagonally through pleasant pine woods, and after a couple of rather indistinct zig-zags arrives on the crest of Carne's south-west ridge, here climbing steeply above craggy ground. The first part of the ridge ascent has been ruined by determined trials motorcyclists (usually local shepherds) but the path improves as the narrower upper section is reached.

The rocky summit turret of the peak can now be seen, and easy walking over an undulating ridge of gravelly limestone brings you to the foot of the final rocks, which can be ascended by a choice of short scrambles.

The summit is delectable. A tiny platform of rock, thrust high above the wooded valleys below, it affords a varied panorama which includes the distant plains of La Vega as well as the nearby peaks of Boca de la Pesca (its fish-head being well seen from here), Cerros Gordo and Huenes, and the abrupt tower of Trevenque, with its long west ridge - the Cuerda (cord) del Trevenque - bounding the deep cleft of the Arroyo del Huenes. There is no convenient alternative way off and descent is best made via the ascent route.

For a longer outing including Carne, see Route 4.

ROUTE 3. ASCENT OF CERRO HUENES FROM CORTIJO SEVILLA VIA FUENTE FRIA

Figures: 13km/460m 4¹/₂-5hrs
Partly MBF

Huenes is the large wooded dome which provides the foreground to the Sierra Nevada when viewed from the vicinity of Granada or Huetor Vega. It overlooks the lower Monachil valley, and presents an unremitting slope of some 800m above the Los Cahorros gorge. Although there is a path from Monachil, ascent by this slope is not recommended!

A far more pleasant way to the top is provided by a long, curling path which starts in the Arroyo del Huenes below the Puente de los Siete Ojos, and works its way around the western flank to the Fuente Fria spring, finally gaining the summit from the east.

Starting from Cortijo Sevilla, it is necessary to walk down the road towards the Puente de los Siete Ojos for 800m to a junction where an apparently drivable track branches left. Shaded parking may be available here, giving the dual advantages of 1.6km less walking, and a cooler car to return to. The branch track descends to cross the stream bed via a small bridge, and shortly narrows to footpath width as it traverses gradually upwards across the western slopes of Cerro del Tamboril. This path gives easy walking, and commands good views over La Zubia and other villages on Granada's southern fringe. The long spur carrying the road from Zubia up through the Pinares de la Zubia to Cumbres Verdes is especially well seen.

Easy angles are maintained until the path reaches the ravine of the Barranco del Lobo, whereupon it makes an abrupt right turn, climbs a short way up the barranco, and then resumes its northerly course. The route soon meanders up into a shady pine wood, and follows a pleasant avenue between the rows of trees (ignore paths branching left and keep on steadily uphill). Arrival at the Cortijo de Fuente Fria is announced by the litter strewn among the trees on your left. The appalling amount of rubbish makes this an unpleasant place - a great pity, because the setting itself, on a sunlit shelf overlooking Monachil, could be lovely (1hr 20min from Cortijo Sevilla).

The path now becomes indistinct, but increasingly green turf leads you south-east, uphill to the spring itself. Travellers who have been smacking their lips in anticipation of a drink from the Fuente Fria (Cold Fountain) are in for a big disappointment. Local farmers, seeing only the practical uses of the water, have piped the outflow into a rusty trough, and a multitude of goats have carpeted the area thickly with droppings - it is better to carry water with you!

From here, a choice of routes is available, but the easiest is to continue south-eastwards on a path which is now distinct once again, passing various farm shacks and goat enclosures, until a thinning of the trees brings the summit outcrops of Huenes into view on the right. Now, things get difficult for mountain bikers. Leave the path and strike uphill directly towards the rocks, gaining the top by one of the many short scrambles which present themselves. Bikers will have to find a route easy enough to carry the bike up (they do exist), or chain the machine to a tree and continue on foot.

The summit consists of a number of rocky tors, the two highest having a tall cairn and a rounded geographical survey column, respectively. The view northward over Monachil and Huetor Vega to the sprawling mass of Granada is spectacular, while to the south, Pico de la Carne is dwarfed by Trevenque, which is in turn humbled by the soaring main ridge, with Veleta and Caballo appearing as small blips on a uniformly high skyline.

The outward route makes a fast and pleasant return, but for alternatives see Route 4 below.

ROUTE 4. CARNE, GORDO, HUENES AND TAMBORIL FROM PUENTE DE LOS SIETE OJOS

Figures: 8km/700m 3¹/₂-4hrs

This round of all the summits of the Huenes massif makes an excellent outing, with varied terrain and views throughout. The route described forms a distorted Q shape on the map due to the ascent and descent being via Carne's south-west ridge - the 'tail' of the Q - but the round of the four tops could be made with equal facility (though rather longer), starting and finishing via Route 3.

For the shorter version, start from the 'seven-eyed' bridge and ascend Pico de la Carne as described in Route 2 above. From the summit, the shaly cone of Cerro Gordo (Fat Hill) can be seen to the north-east. Scramble down Carne's northern rocks and slither down rather unpleasant gravelly grooves to a col (1765m) from where a choice of paths snake along the sides and over the tops of subsidiary hillocks in the direction of Gordo's southern 'ridge'. The small conical summit of Gordo is easily reached via a gravel path directly up this ridge.

Cerro Gordo (1894m) is a featureless hill, resembling a pile of small stones deposited by some immense dump truck, but its summit is a fine viewpoint for the complex topography of the upper Monachil valley and its tributaries, as well as the ridge leading eastwards to Cerro de la Cortijuela and Pico del Tesoro, with the Peñones de San Francisco and Veleta dominating the skyline. A descent northwards leads via a broad col to a secondary top at 1855m giving a good view of the route to Huenes.

From this point, Huenes appears as a low whaleback of crag,

surrounded by trees. The best approach is a bee-line (sketchy paths) across limestone scrubland towards the left (west) edge of the rocks. As the broad saddle below the summit rocks is reached, the terrain changes dramatically. Pleasant shady trees, and luxuriant green turf are suddenly encountered, giving the atmosphere of a walk in the park. A complete contrast to the arid landscape just traversed. Strolling pleasantly up the green slope brings you to the foot of the final rocks near the foot of an easy gully - liberally decorated with goat droppings - which leads directly onto the summit area.

The next objective, Cerro del Tamboril, is clearly in view almost due south but don't be tempted into a bee-line or you will fall foul of the deep rift of the Barranco del Lobo. Instead, descend the little gully used for the ascent, then make a wide arc around the head of the Barranco, eventually approaching Tamboril from the east. En route, another change of terrain is encountered when tussocky grass, reminiscent of England's Pennine moors, is traversed as the head of the ravine is skirted, but this soon reverts to the limestone, scrub, and prickly vegetation typical of this area. A straightforward scramble takes you to the top of Tamboril's summit cone at 1776m.

The view from here is similar to that from Pico de la Carne, except that Boca de la Pesca's resemblance to an upturned fish-head is, if anything, even more marked.

From here, make towards the obvious but unnamed peak (1786m) seen to the left of Pico de la Carne, crossing rough scrubby vegetation around the head of the Barranco de las Majadillas. Traversing or skirting this minor hillock brings you onto the col below Carne, the summit of which can be avoided if desired by a contouring path branching right about halfway up the final ridge. However, the peaked top is so good that you will probably prefer to enjoy it for a second time, especially if it is late in the day - it makes a wonderful perch from which to savour a glorious Spanish dusk, prior to a leisurely descent into the cool shadows of the valley, and a 'cerveza' or two.

ROUTE 5. ASCENT OF TREVENQUE FROM CORTIJO SEVILLA VIA CUERDA DEL TREVENQUE

Figures: 9km/700m 2¹/₂-3hrs
Partly MBF

The long west ridge, or 'Cuerda', of Trevenque bounds the southern side of the Huenes valley and provides the classic route up this striking limestone peak. The purity of the ridge has been spoiled to a certain extent by a jeep track cut into its southern flank close to the crest, but although now impassable to four-wheeled vehicles due to water erosion, this track will be regarded as a boon by mountain bikers. The track is continuous right to the foot of the final pyramid at about 1825m, and although cycling up it may prove hard labour, it would provide a blissfully easy descent. Despite the intrusion of the track, this is still a more enjoyable way up the peak than the short, steep struggle to the top from the east (Route 6).

From the parking area near Cortijo Sevilla, the track commences beside the concrete channel carrying the Canal de la Espartera, a hydro-electric waterway taking water from La Toma (The Taking) in the Dilar valley, and transporting it to a point just beyond Boca de la Pesca from where it plunges 400m down a pipe to drive the turbines of the Central Eléctrica de Dilar.

Walkers can take a more direct path seen rising diagonally across the slope ahead, and avoid the initial long zig-zag of the jeep track, but mountain bikers are advised to stick to the track's easier gradient. Both routes rejoin at a small sandy ridge, where the path from Las Arenales (Route 7) also converges. From here, the route to the summit 'tower' could not be more obvious. Both the track and the ridge are well defined, the former occupying a shelf which scribes a relentless uphill line towards the looming pyramid, the latter forming a narrow switchback of small, gravelly peaks. Take your pick!

At the foot of the final craggy upthrust, the track swings off to the right, to a sudden dead end overlooking the sandy area called Las Arenales. There are a number of ways ahead from here, but whichever you choose, aim for the obvious green slope in the middle of the face. This leads easily to a gap in the shattered crest of the south-east ridge. Pass over the ridge via this convenient gap, and clamber up easy rock steps on the eastern side to the summit.

The actual top consists of a number of rock turrets clustered tightly together, some of them so small that a head for heights is required to stand upright on their highest points - a proper mountain top. In common with many peaks in the Sierra Nevada, one of the summit rocks carries the name of the peak along with its height in metres and an unintelligible slogan in red paint. A long red and white pole with a red flag is sometimes found crowning the top, but sometimes it is absent. Perhaps it is the work of the mysterious 'Friends of Trevenque'?

This is truly a grand eyrie. Trevenque, at 2079m is decisively higher than any of its neighbours, giving the climber on its summit a wondrous panorama over all the subservient peaks. Veleta, 1300m higher, is too distant to assert any authority, and Trevenque stands aloof from the rest of the Cumbres Verdes. No wonder it has been referred to as El Pico Rey (The King Peak).

For variety, a descent via Las Arenales is a possibility worth considering, but there is no quicker or more direct way back to Cortijo Sevilla than the way you came.

ROUTE 6. ASCENT OF TREVENQUE FROM COLLADO DEL TREVENQUE

Figures: 1.6km/240m Under 1hr

This is the shortest and quickest route up Trevenque, and also the steepest. On the Huenes forestry road (RG9), after passing Casa Cortijuela, the track begins to climb towards the Huenes/Dilar watershed. At the end of a short straight with Trevenque looming directly ahead, the track turns left and climbs more steeply. On this left-hand bend a small track branches downhill on the right (blocked with a pile of earth to prevent vehicle access). This is the best starting point.

The little branch track leads in 50m to a small clearing, where the route becomes obvious. A gravelly path leads over a minor hillock to climb directly up the facing ridge into an obvious weakness in Trevenque's eastern facade. The climb is loose and stony, but leads straight to the top in around 30mins.

ROUTE 7. TOMA DEL CANAL AND LAS ARENALES FROM CORTIJO SEVILLA

Figures: 14km/550m (incl. ascent of Puntal de los Mecheros)
MBF

Good views of the Dilar valley, Los Alayos, and Trevenque are provided by this simple and enjoyable route. From the parking area at Cortijo Sevilla, cross the concrete channel of the Espartera hydro-electrical canal, and head downhill in a south-easterly direction with the farm ruins below on the right. In 100m a good path will be picked up, traversing across the steep slopes into the Dilar valley.

This path is excellent. Broad and smooth, it makes for easy and scenic walking (or biking) as it traverses high above the river with many picturesque viewpoints. After looping through the startling ravine of the Barranco del Búho (búho = owl), the path descends through sparse forest, largely destroyed by fires in 1991, to a junction where the path to Casa Rosales branches left. Keep right at this fork and follow the undulating path across flatter terrain crossing a dirt road, which was built in 1992, until it emerges by a small pumping station at river level.

The path now becomes narrower as it threads its way upstream amid luxuriant vegetation, soon reaching the house and, just beyond, the small dam of La Toma del Canal where the water for the Dilar hydro-electrical station is taken from the river. It is possible to penetrate further upstream, even to reach the goat trading station at the Collado de la Chaquetas (see below) but this involves rough terrain, and a certain amount of wading - one for the adventurous.

Less intrepid travellers should return to the pumping station and clamber up the steep slopes behind it on a small path, crossing the canal en route (partly enclosed) and reach the 1992 dirt road. To avoid carrying, bikers may prefer to return down the valley path to reach the dirt road at a lower level.

Trevenque and Collado de Chaquetas from the slopes of Puntal de los Mecheros

This relatively new track may now be followed as it climbs out of the valley in long zig-zags, passing the ruined and graffiti-daubed Casa Rosales, and higher up, a new hut. The track leads to

61

Trevenque from Las Arenales. Photo by Ian Roberts

the Collado de la Chaquetas, adjacent to which is the 1872m peak of Puntal de los Mecheros, an undistinguished summit which is worth climbing just for the view of the Dilar valley. Another advantage of visiting the col is that drinking water is available from the adjacent farm buildings, which serve as a goat trading post.

View savoured and thirst slaked, retrace your steps down the dirt road for 800m until just beyond the bed of the obvious stream gully (Barranco de Aguas Blanquillas). A good path, marked with paint splashes, branches off right, traversing slopes high above the Dilar valley to cross a narrow col in Trevenque's secondary west ridge and enter the desert landscape of Las Arenales (The Sands).

This broad sand-filled valley - actually the upper reaches of the Barranco del Búho - would be an ideal location for filming a western. All that's required is Clint Eastwood, and some tumbleweed blowing by. Standing majestically at the head of the barranco is Trevenque, with its switchback 'Cuerda' ridge bounding the far side of the hollow and the curious limestone thumb known as La Esfinge (The Sphinx) poking out of the upper sands.

Follow the bed of the valley 'downstream' walking in soft white

Collado de Ruquino and Trevenque from the Tesoro pinnacle

sand (which reflects the heat of the summer sun like a mirror) until it begins to narrow. As you approach the obvious rocky defile of the lower ravine (crossed earlier) look out for the paint-marked path which reappears, climbing out of the sand on the right. This path now ascends to rendezvous with the jeep track and the path from the Cuerda del Trevenque (Route 5), either of which can then be followed down to the starting point at Cortijo Sevilla col.

THE PICO DEL TESORO RIDGE

The northern side of the Arroyo del Huenes is bounded by two massifs, separated by a pronounced col (El Collado). West of El Collado stands the Huenes group, with Carne and Gordo (see above). To the east lies a long ridge with many small peaks, culminating in the shapely pyramid of Pico del Tesoro (Peak of Treasure) at 1995m. Beyond, the ridge falls to the pleasant green saddle of the Collado de Matas Verdes, dividing Tesoro from the Loma de Dilar which leads up to the distant Veleta.

ROUTE 8. PICO DEL TESORO, CERRO DE LA CORTIJUELA AND CERRO DEL COCÓN FROM CASA DE LA CORTIJUELA (on Huenes Valley road - RG9)

Figures: 9km/650m (with return via Collado de Matas Verdes)

The Casa Forestal de la Cortijuela (simply 'Cortijuela' to most local people) is a delectable spot from which to start a walk. With its shady trees, grassy bank and delicious 'fuente', it is so delectable that there is a risk of not starting at all!

Convince yourself that the pleasures of this location will be better enjoyed after the walk, and set out north-east from the fuente, striking directly up towards the trees at right-angles to the road. A good path appears almost immediately, and leads pleasantly up through the forest to the Collado de Matas Verdes (Col of Green Shrubs) with its ramshackle fence. A striking view of the San Francisco ridge of Veleta and the scars of the Sierra Nevada road and ski development now appears across the Monachil valley.

Climbing Cerro Gordo with Pico de la Carne behind. (Route 4)

From Cerro del Tamboril. Carne, overtopped by Trevenque, overtopped by the snowy main ridge
Trevenque and Los Alayos de Dilar from the slopes of Cerro del Cocón

Pico del Tesoro (1995m) is the obvious peak to the left (north-west) of the collado, and is easily gained by rough slopes keeping to the left side of the ridge crest to avoid craggy upthrusts. Cortijuela to summit: 1hr. The summit is formed of three distinct outcrops, with a hollow of prickly vegetation in between, and much evidence of Cabra Montes. In fact, this whole ridge seems to be a favourite with the mountain goats, and an evening visit can often be rewarded with some very close encounters with sizeable groups of these surefooted creatures.

A descent south-west over slopes of loose limestone and spiny plants brings you to a prominent rock finger overlooking the grassy Collado de Ruquino. From here, the ridge over Cerro de la Cortijuela to El Collado and Cerro del Cocón is well seen, with a rough jeep track traversing its northern slopes to cross the crest at El Collado. This 'jeep' track, which is now impassable to four-wheeled vehicles, affords a convenient and quick return from Cerro del Cocón to Collado de Ruquino.

Descend to the col and climb directly ahead over a grassy hump to pass under a band of low trees, scrambling up an easy little gully to emerge on the crest of the Cortijuela ridge. This section is the highlight of the route. The ridge is only short, and nowhere difficult, but is a delightful succession of little limestone turrets, with superb views and many places which tempt you just to sit and soak up the tranquillity of these quiet hills.

When the ridge widens to a broad whaleback, traverse the next broad hump and descend to the jeep track, which can then be followed to El Collado. Alternatively, it is not too difficult to continue along the ridge over two further minor summits, reaching El Collado directly from the south.

Cerro del Cocón (1858m) thrusts its prominent cone skyward directly above El Collado (1786m) entailing a few minutes' hard labour up its steep gravelly slopes, but it is worth it. The summit is one of the gems of Baja Montaña. The conical slopes culminate in a tiny rounded-off peak, giving superb views of Cerro Gordo, Huenes, the Monachil valley and, looking back, Pico del Tesoro and Trevenque, overtopped by the soaring skyline of Veleta and the main ridge. Truly a place to linger.

Cocón's secondary summit can be seen to the east, and this is easily visited in 10min.

Returning to the collado, the jeep track affords an easy return to Collado de Ruquino, from where a good path descends southward to approach Cortijuela via a steep slope alongside the imposing crag (not marked on maps) which overlooks the house. This is the most logical and scenic end to the walk, but there are possible variations.

The first of these is a small path, which forks right (south) from the track at the first col after leaving El Collado. This col is easily identified by two prominent, but small, conical peaks flanking the track at this point. The path leads down through the woods to join the Huenes valley forestry road (RG9) less than a kilometre from Cortijuela.

The second variation is a path commencing at the Ruquino col and contouring the southern slopes of Pico del Tesoro to emerge on the Collado de Matas Verdes, from where a descent by the outward route can be made.

ROUTE 9. ASCENT OF CERRO DEL MIRADOR FROM CASA DE LA CORTIJUELA

Figures: 4.5km/362m
MBF

Although it overtops all the peaks of the western Baja Montaña barring Trevenque, this hill is really only a bump on the side of the huge Loma de Dilar, which leads up eventually to Veleta. It cannot be compared with lower, but much shapelier peaks such as Tesoro, Carne, or even Boca de La Pesca. However, as its name suggests, it is an excellent viewpoint for the upper Monachil valley, and it is easily reached from Collado de Matas Verdes (see above) in 30min. From the collado, simply follow the fence south-east and east to a broad col (wrongly marked as Collado del Pino on IGN map), then cross the fence to reach the 2062m summit.

LOS ALAYOS DE DILAR (Highest point 1978m)

The Alayos de Dilar vie with Trevenque for the title of 'most striking feature of Baja Montaña'. The name refers to a long ridge bounding the south side of the Dilar valley - actually the lower end of the Loma de Peñamadura - which contains a number of summits, the highest of which is one of the many tops of Los Castillejos. The best known of the Alayos, though, is without doubt the unusual double summit of Corazón de la Sandía (Heart of the Watermelon) (1886m). The highest of the two summits is a simple shaly cone on the main ridge, but the second summit juts out above the Dilar valley like a huge rock melon - hence the name.

Access to the Alayos is not straightforward, and the ridge does not lend itself easily to a circular route. Those described below are probably the most logical ways of 'bagging' Los Alayos.

ROUTE 10. CORAZÓN DE LA SANDÍA FROM LOS MIRADORES

Figures: 9km/590m (with return via traversing path)

On the eastern fringe of the clearing at Los Miradores (see RG10) a good, clear path commences and winds its way up into the forest.

After crossing a wide dry barranco the path climbs in well engineered zig-zags, with occasional short-cut paths to emerge on the ridge crest just below the summit of Picacho Alto. From here the crest of the ridge can be followed over the Picacho, and various rocky peaks in an interesting traverse, leading directly to the double top of Corazón de la Sandía.

The easy conical top (which is the highest) forms part of the main ridge, but it is the unusual rock 'melon' jutting out over the Dilar valley which makes the peak special. To reach its top, cross the narrow col between the two summits and scramble up various ledges, with much route choice, and a small degree of exposure to the rocky crest.

The route is very short and not difficult, and an effort should be made to overcome any fear of the exposed bits - this top is worth bagging! The view over the Dilar valley from the summit is spectacular, with Trevenque and its Cuerda being particularly well seen.

There is nothing to be said against returning along the ridge, but if a variation is required, there is a traversing path running along the northern slopes which is easily reached. Retrace your steps along the ridge, passing over the unnamed summit adjacent to El Corazón. At the next col, it is an easy matter to make a descent to the path which will lead you easily back to the wide col below Picacho Alto and thus to the zig-zag path back to Los Miradores.

ROUTE 11. CORAZÓN DE LA SANDÍA FROM CORTIJO SEVILLA

Figures: 14km/690m (out and back by described route)

From the Cortijo Sevilla parking area, take the descending path into the Dilar valley, which passes through the Barranco del Búho and crosses the broad slopes on the northern side of the valley, an area once thickly wooded, but now denuded due to forest fires in 1991 (see Route 7).

After passing across the bulldozed track, the path converges on the river bed, finally reaching it just before a small but prominent pumphouse. Exactly at the point where the path comes alongside the river (here hidden under trees, with a dry oxbow next to the path) another path branches off indistinctly to the right. This path fords the river under a low tunnel of foliage, then becomes distinct as it climbs up through the forest in loops and zig-zags. After about 10min of steady walking, a slightly obscure junction branches right between bushes to climb out of the trees and mount quite steeply onto the northern flank of the Los Alayos ridge (see also Route 13 below).

This is the path which traverses the entire length of the ridge, climbing and descending over many subsidiary ridges, and finally crossing the crest at the western end and descending to the clearing at Los Miradores.

There are a number of possible routes to the summit of Corazón de la Sandía from various points on this path, but it's probably best to continue until directly below the distinctive rock melon, then work up a steep gully on rough ground to emerge on the ridge next to the summit, from where it is an easy matter to scramble up the final rocks to the top.

A number of alternative return routes are possible; see Routes 10, 12, and 13.

ROUTE 12. LOS CASTILLEJOS FROM COLLADO DE CHAQUETAS

Figures: 11km/420m (out and back via described route)

Below the farm buildings at Collado de Chaquetas (see RG9), a once distinct path, now rough and partially obscured by scree, descends to the river bed and a small footbridge. From here the path becomes more obvious, climbing diagonally across the steep slopes on the east side of the river. Ignore indistinct branches trending upwards to the left, and continue along the main path as it levels out and traverses along the flank of the Loma de Peña Madura, heading for the obvious col at the eastern end of Los Alayos, with only minor uphill sections.

Skirting beneath the crags of Cerro del Espinar (a minor outcrop on the side of the main ridge), the path encounters a ramshackle fence barring the way. However, the farmer has thoughtfully provided a makeshift 'gate' which can be unhooked to continue.

The path now turns northward, towards the pine trees at the top of the Cuesta del Pina, but about halfway between the gate and the pines, a forked junction with a path joining from the left is reached. Turn sharp left here to head back in almost the direction you came but at a higher level. This path will lead you to the Collado del Pino.

The route to the summits of Los Castillejos is now obvious, climbing a distinct ridge to the west. On reaching the ridge, a number of routes are possible. The whole crest is a succession of rock towers, with a network of tiny paths linking or avoiding them. Choose your summits according to your scrambling expertise or head for heights.

The only logical return to Collado de Chaquetas is by the outward route, but it is possible to descend Cuesta del Pino to Toma del Canal, then climb up to the col via Cortijo Rosales (see Routes 7, 10, and 13).

ROUTE 13. INTEGRAL DE LOS ALAYOS FROM CORTIJO SEVILLA (full traverse)

Figures: 21-23km/900-1000m (depending on ridge-route chosen)

This route, one of the 'classics' of Sierra Nevada, makes a superb day out, but should not be underestimated. The terrain on the ridge is very time-consuming, and the traversing path, used for the return, is long and has many ups and downs. A full day should be allowed, and in summer it is imperative to carry sufficient water because there is no 'agua potable' on the entire route. However, with a little planning, and a fair measure of grim determination, a great day out can be had on this rugged ridge.

Starting from the Cortijo Sevilla parking, follow Route 7 to the indistinct path junction near the pumphouse (see also Route 11). From here, take the path crossing the stream, which enters the pine forest, and ascends the Cuesta del Pino, to emerge from the trees a short distance before the Collado del Pino. Shortly, you will reach a fork in the path, the left branch heading slightly downhill to lead eventually to the Collado de Chaquetas (see RG9 and Route 12), the right branch leading up to the Collado del Pino, at the eastern end of Los Alayos.

The ridge is now obvious, offering a wealth of route choice, with some 14 individual tops to be visited or bypassed according to your individual fitness, expertise, courage or sense of purity. After visiting however many tops your conscience, bravery, or determination dictates, you will arrive on the western side of Picacho Alto, overlooking the broad saddle of Los Miradores (see RG10 and Route 10), where you can join the excellent path to return along the northern face of the ridge.

This path begins as an easy smooth path cut into the steep slope, but after rounding the head of the impressive Rambla Seca, it makes a long zig-zag descent to a much lower level. After crossing a low col, the path descends further still, eventually joining the bed of a small dry barranco. Do not continue down this barranco. Shortly after reaching the gully, another path branches off to the right (large tree at the junction) and climbs back up towards the ridge, crossing another subsidiary spur, before descending and traversing around to the foot of yet another zig-zag climb onto a shallow col below Pico de la Virgen. The worst of the climbing is now over, and the path descends into the forest to join the outward route on the Cuesta del Pino, which can be descended to the Rio Dilar at the pumphouse. Now all that remains is to retrace your steps along the north side of the valley to Cortijo Sevilla.

ROUTE 14. A CIRCUIT OF EL TREVENQUE FROM CORTIJO SEVILLA

Figures: 16.5km/600m (with finish via lower valley path)
MBF

Although it is quite possible to walk this route and enjoy it, it is better suited to a traverse by mountain bike. The first half of the route is on the broad gravel road in the Arroyo del Huenes (RG9). This track is pleasantly shaded and sees very few cars except on Sundays, when the valley is invaded by the 'Domingeros' (Sunday people).

Follow the road as described in RG9 until the Collado de la Chaquetas is reached. From here, continue past the chain barrier, descending on a still good dirt road which descends via a new refugio (locked and shuttered), to the old derelict Casa Rosales. From here, two alternatives present themselves. Either continue down the road until almost at the river, and join the lower of the two valley paths towards Cortijo Sevilla, or leave the road at the point of the zig-zag which encloses the Casa Rosales (there's a large threshing platform at this point), joining the higher footpath which leads across the slopes to join the Cortijo Sevilla path before Barranco del Búho. It is also possible to return from Collado de la Chaquetas via Las Arenales (see Route 7).

71

PART THREE

Alta Montaña (High Mountains)

INTRODUCTION

The high tops of the Sierra Nevada have a character, and a seriousness, which contrasts markedly with the miniature peaks of Baja Montaña. During summer, the two highest tops have easy access thanks to the Sierra Nevada road, South Sierra Nevada road (RG2, RG15), and the Mulhacén summit road, and their summits can often be crowded with family parties who have come up for the day by car. I have seen an ordinary Citroën AX on the rough car park near Mulhacén's top, so it is possible, with determined driving, to bag the two highest peaks without walking more than 300yds.

However, many of the other high summits are considerably more difficult to reach, either because of their remoteness or their arduous terrain. Almost all of the 3000m zone is exceptionally rough, with long ridges of shattered boulders flanked by broken crags ('tajos'). To avoid the crags it is necessary to tackle steep gullies of sliding scree, and at this altitude, under a hot sun, high levels of both fitness and fortitude are prerequisites of any ascents of the more remote peaks.

Winter brings a different set of circumstances. The weather is more unpredictable, and has potential for extreme severity, and with the Sierra Nevada Roads closed above 2000m the seriousness of any expedition is increased considerably. Having accepted these facts, and prepared for them, you will be in a position to enjoy perhaps the best mountaineering season of all in the Sierra Nevada. In good conditions, with well settled snow and a clear sky (encouragingly common), the ascents of Veleta, Mulhacén and Alcazaba, or the traverse of Tajos de la Virgen, Neveros and Altos, are classic expeditions comparable with routes in the Alps or Pyrenees.

(A) ROUTES FROM THE GENIL VALLEY

The valley of the Genil drains the northern faces of the main ridge, the narrow V-shaped ravine leading via numerous branches to spectacular 'corrals' beneath the northern crags of Alcazaba, Mulhacén, Crestones de Rio Seco and Veleta. Progressing up the valley road (RG3) from Maitena, the first major bifurcation occurs at the site of the old San Juan tranvia station, now the roadhead. At this point, the Barranco de San Juan branches off. This Barranco (which has no worthwhile routes for walkers) penetrates high into the northern slopes of Veleta, but then ends in a mild bowl known as the Hoya de la Mora, below the Sierra Nevada Road (RG1/RG2).

Further progress up the main valley is by the old miners' track called the Vereda de la Estrella (Footpath of the Stars), which is described below. In another $2^{1}/_{2}$kms the Rio Vadillo branches off on the northern side, defining the Loma del Calvario, which leads up to broad slopes below El Cuervo. The next major branch valley is that of the Rio Guarnón, which leads up into the superb Corral del Veleta, where Europe's most southerly glacier survived until early this century. Dividing the San Juan and Guarnón valleys is the long ridge of the Loma de San Juan.

The Rio Genil now becomes the Rio Real, curving southward around the toe of the Loma del Lanchar to the final major bifurcation. Here, the valley forks. The left fork forms the Rio Valdecasillas which culminates in the grand corral of Hoya del Mulhacén beneath the looming north faces of Mulhacén and Alcazaba, while the right fork becomes the Rio Valdeinfiernos, leading to the wild Corral de Valdeinfiernos, below the jagged Crestones de Rio Seco. The central ridge between these two is the Loma de Casillas, which leads up to the 3000m peaks of Juego Bolos, and Puntal de la Caldera. Apart from the San Juan barranco, which has impenetrable vegetation, all these ravines and their dividing ridges can be used to approach the high summits.

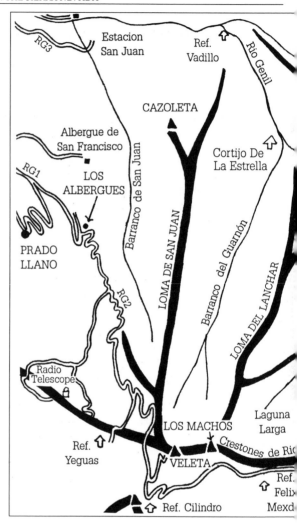

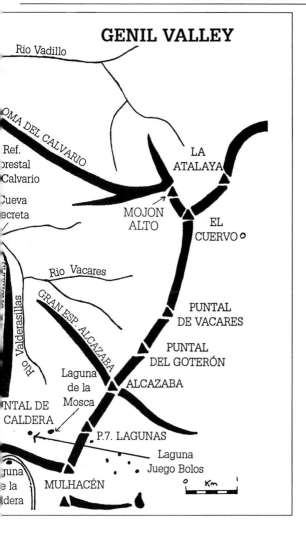

ROUTE 15. THE VEREDA DE LA ESTRELLA. FROM SAN JUAN TO CUEVA SECRETA

Figures: 9.5km/600m (excluding return)
MBF

The roadhead at the old Estacion de San Juan (RG3) is the usual starting point for the Vereda, even though the path actually starts further down the valley, a little above the Bar Chiquito. Directly opposite the station building is the mouth of the Barranco de San Juan, and this area is a popular resort with 'Domingeros' on summer Sundays, so much so that the small parking area is often full, and chaos reigns as cars attempt to return down valley and are met by cars coming up. Passing on the slightly precipitous and very narrow track is an awkward operation. You have been warned!

From the San Juan parking area, cross the little footbridge over the Genil into the mouth of the Barranco and join the Vereda, which climbs leftwards up a small rocky outcrop onto the steep southern slope of the Genil valley. The path is broad and distinct, and climbs purposefully up through attractive woods to a higher level, with a couple of zig-zags to help ease the gradient. At the top of this initial pull, the path emerges on a broad terrace high above the river, which is only occasionally glimpsed threading its way along the deep and narrow slot at the valley bed. Note the supporting walls, and man-made rock gateways which betray the Vereda's origins as a well engineered miners' track leading to the Minas de la Estrella and Minas de Justicia high in the upper reaches of the valley.

Rising and falling gently, the path continues easily along this high terrace, winding its way in and out of various minor side valleys. In about 1hr, a junction is reached (indistinct paint marks on rocks). The path to the Cuesta de los Presidiarios plunges downhill to the Vadillo Hut by the river (see Route 16). The Vereda continues at its previous high level and in 5min turns a corner to be confronted by a stunning view of the north faces of Alcazaba and Mulhacén, best seen in April when the air is less hazy, and snow drapes the peaks. This spot is known as the 'Mirador' (viewpoint), and is a popular bivouac site (signs of camp fires in the middle of the path).

From here, the Vereda continues easily for a further hour until the ruined buildings of the Cortijo de la Estrella are reached at the confluence of the Rios Guarnón and Real. The Rio Real is the continuation of the main (Genil) valley, while the long straight trench of the Rio Guarnón drains the Veleta corral. See Route 20 for details of approaches to the high summits via the Guarnón valley.

The Vereda narrows and loops down and across the Guarnón via a small bridge, then climbs up into the narrow ravine of the Rio Real, now following the river quite closely. A further hour brings you to the final major bifurcation of the valley, passing the ruins of the Minas de la Justicia en route. At this final junction the Loma de las Casillas rises steeply directly ahead. The minor Barranco de Lucía enters from the left, very close to the Rio Valdecasillas, here debouching from a narrow opening between steep slopes. The right branch - the Rio Valdeinfiernos - carries the path, which is now much more indistinct, as it twists right and then left to emerge in an open area with grassy swards, a huge boulder with small 'cave' beneath, and the inevitable litter. This is the popular bivouac/camping site known as the Cueva Secreta.

Approximately $3^{1}/_{2}$hrs walking from San Juan, proportionately less by mountain bike.

ROUTE 16. ASCENTS OF EL CUERVO, VACARES OR ALCAZABA FROM VADILLO HUT

Figures: 28km/2400m (to Alcazaba and back via Route 16b)

The Vadillo bivouac hut stands on the south bank of the Rio Genil, adjacent to the confluence with the Rio Vadillo. It is reached via the Vereda de la Estrella (Route 15 above).

Rising steeply above the hut, and dividing the valleys of the Genil and the Vadillo, is the ridge called the Loma del Calvario, which broadens rapidly as it gains height, finally forming the rather shapeless 3000m summits of Mojon Alto and El Cuervo. These two tops are hardly worth the effort of the long climb from the Vadillo (which entails almost 1900m of ascent), but the attraction is the access to the rugged escarpment of Puntal de Vacares and Puntal del Goteron, which leads in turn to Alcazaba - one of the most spectacular summits of the range.

From the refugio, cross the concrete footbridge (Puente del Burro) over the Genil, and pick up a good path rising quite steeply through the trees on the flank of the ridge in a south-easterly direction. This path has many variations caused by walkers shortcutting the original zig-zags. At approximately 1600m, a branch to the right leads out of the trees to climb below a line of crag with excellent views of the high summits across the profound trench of the Genil valley. The left branch trends back through the forest to reach the ridge crest at about 1700m. Both paths converge at a wide grassy terrace with freshwater springs and basic stone building - the Refugio Forestal del Calvarios (1900m). This is a popular camping place, and would make a convenient point at which to break the climb if ascending from San Juan. Near to the refugio are the ruins of the Choza del Tio Papeles, an earlier hut now in ruins and, of course, strewn with litter.

From here, paths are at best indistinct or discontinuous, but it is fairly straightforward to climb up to the ridge crest (if heading for El Cuervo or Vacares), or to traverse around the broad slopes above the headwaters of the Rio Vacares (if heading for Alcazaba).

ROUTE 16(a). TO THE CUNETA DE VACARES, CUERVO AND VACARES

From the Refugio Forestal, make a gradual rising traverse towards the highest visible point on the broad hump of El Cuervo; small paths will be seen, but these are mainly goat-tracks, and generally lead nowhere. Keep heading in a south-easterly direction until the Cuneta de Vacares appears as a pronounced col between the Cuervo and Vacares summits. It is now an easy matter to make a bee-line across increasingly rough and barren terrain to reach the col. Obvious bivouac sites in this vicinity are the work of parties attempting the Integral de los Tres Mil Metros (Route 45). It is possible to make the ascent of Alcazaba from this point by following the ridge over the crests of Vacares and Goteron to the foot of the final pyramid, then using one of the routes described below.

ROUTE 16(b). TO TAJOS DEL GOTERON AND ALCAZABA

The high col between Alcazaba and Puntal del Goteron is clearly seen from the Refugio Forestal. This col is the key to the ascent of the peak from this side for walkers. Alcazaba (The Citadel) is a very aggressive mountain, being ringed by huge crags on three sides. The only 'easy' routes are those from the south, and any attempt on the summit from the west, east, or north requires the crags to be climbed or circumvented via scree gullies and terraces. Competant scramblers can find a way up the north face without too much difficulty by utilising the obvious shelf crossing the face at approximately 3000m (the Gran Vasar). From this shelf, a number of routes are possible via the network of buttresses and scree chutes which comprise the face. However, anywhere on this face is an exposed situation, and the scree gullies can be extremely unpleasant. Winter is a different matter entirely. Then, the scree gullies become superb snow-climbs requiring the expertise and equipment of the alpinist.

For the walker, the ascent involves a big detour around the toe of the long overhanging crag bounding the mountain's north-east side (Tajos del Goteron) and then a long drag up broad but steep scree and boulder slopes to the summit. To reach the crag from the Refugio Forestal, head south-east from the hut, skirting the headwaters of the Rio Vacares (a tributary of the Valdecasillas) on a small path. As the looming walls of the peak are approached, keep left to scramble up scree and loose rocks and emerge on the ridge close to Puntal del Goteron. It is then easy to follow the main crest to a point below the big ridge step, which is actually the end of the Tajos del Goteron. The best route from here is to hug the base of the crag - there is a possibility of obtaining drinking water from the permanent meltwater which descends from permanent snowfields ('ventisqueros') above. Eventually, the cliff subsides into scree, and it is then straightforward, though laborious, to climb up onto the ridge and follow it to the 3366m summit.

ROUTE 17. THE ASCENT OF MULHACÉN FROM CUEVA SECRETA

Figures: 14km/1780m (out and back via El Corredor)

From the litter-strewn grass of the Cueva Secreta bivouac area the north walls of Mulhacén, Puntal de la Caldera, and the Crestones de Rio Seco are ranged across the skyline. The only obvious line is the long ridge leading to the 3023m summit of Juego de Bolos, which links with Puntal de la Caldera - the Loma de la Casillas. However, there are other more interesting ways of scaling the Pared Norte - even for walkers.

The bivouac site is actually situated in the valley of the Rio Valdeinfiernos, which leads up into the grand Corral de Valdeinfiernos, and, via a tributary, to the Laguna Larga - both below the long serrated Crestones de Rio Seco, but it is also the usual starting point for the ascent of Mulhacén via the valley of the Rio Valdecasillas. A good path climbs over the lower part of the Loma de la Casillas into the Valdecasillas valley, ascending towards the picturesque waterfalls falling from the Hoya del Mulhacén, the hanging valley below the mountain's north face.

The path maintains an easy gradient for most of its ascent, steepening only when it reaches the final headwall of the valley, where it ascends by linking three sloping shelves alongside the cascades to reach the mouth of the Hoya. From here, the Pared Norte of Mulhacén is severely foreshortened, appearing as a squat arc of rock and scree. There is little impression of its true height of almost 700m from screes to summit. In the bed of the Hoya lies the Laguna de la Mosca, surrounded by soft grass - an oasis of green where all around is arid scree and rock. This would make an ideal bivouac site if tackling the climb in two stages - as many people will.

The Hoya del Mulhacén is surrounded by high rock walls. The north-western face of Alcazaba continues as a lofty crag below the insignificant blip of the Puntal de las Siete Lagunas, leading into the massive buttresses of Mulhacén's Pared Norte, which in turn merge with the crags of Puntal de la Caldera. Only at the Collado del Mulhacén - between Mulhacén and Caldera - is there an obvious path out of the huge bowl. This path can be used to gain access to the easy west flank if the easiest option is required. There is, however, a direct path for walkers giving access to the Cañada de las Siete Lagunas and the foot of Mulhacén's north-eastern ridge. El Corredor is a series of easy but loose scree gullies which provide a surprisingly easy way up what appears to be an impregnable cliff. This is a more challenging way to the top, and leaves the west flank route for an easy return to the Hoya.

Looking up from below, directly beneath the col between Puntal de las Siete Lagunas and Mulhacén, you will see three obvious left-trending 'rakes' which penetrate about 70m up the rock wall. The middle one is the key to El Corredor. Scramble up the obvious scree cone to the foot of this rake, and then ascend it until you emerge atop the rock buttress which bounds the lower edge of the gully. Ahead is a deep cleft, but by doubling back to the right another simple scree slope presents itself, enabling you to circumvent a looming buttress above and gain the final broad slopes of loose rocks which lead out onto the ridge above the Cañada de las Siete Lagunas.

From here, the summit of Puntal de las Siete Lagunas can be easily reached in less than 5min. Mulhacén is a rather harder option. Looking up at the final ridge, the crest is obviously impracticable as it vaults upward in a series of shattered buttresses and slabs - unpleasant even for climbers. The walkers' option is to use the obvious broad scree gully to the left of the ridge-step. This gully is a trail of patience in summer when there is no snow and the scree is at its most detestable. At other times of year it may be filled with snow of varying consistencies from easy, soft mush to a smooth slope of hard névé, necessitating crampons and axe for safety. In full winter conditions, the whole route from the Hoya del Mulhacén becomes a serious mountaineering expedition.

Ascend the gully, which begins broadly, then splits into two narrower ones. Either of the upper branches will lead you onto a more solid area of jagged rocks and it is then possible to move back rightwards onto the crest of the ridge. The remainder of the ascent is over huge slabs and blocks on the broad shattered crest, with spectacular views down the Pared Norte at various points.

The summit has a small shrine, a 5m high iron cross (sometimes knocked over - presumably by those who have come up to the top of the summit road only 10min walk away), and the ruins of a number of small, but at one time quite solid, buildings. These buildings were put up in 1879 as part of a survey by the Comisión Geodésica during which triangulation measurements were made of various points in Spain and Algeria. This survey fixed Mulhacén's altitude as 3481m - the highest summit on the Iberian Peninsula - and this height is still widely accepted today.

As mentioned above, the west flank provides an easy descent to the Collado del Mulhacén, from where a distinct path winds its way down to the Laguna de la Mosca.

ROUTE 18. THE ASCENT OF PUNTAL DE LA CALDERA VIA LOMA DE LAS CASILLAS FROM CUEVA SECRETA

Figures: 10km/1500m (up and down)

Follow the main Valdecasillas/Mulhacén path up to the low col in the ridge (Majada del Palo), then branch rightwards to follow the crest. The path on the ridge is indistinct but the crest is well defined and impossible to lose. This is a very long and arduous ascent, but the unfolding views of the vast northern escarpment of the range are spectacular, and make the effort worthwhile.

A detailed description is almost superfluous. It is simply a matter of following the ridge as it vaults endlessly upward. In the later stages, there are some steep sections, and a little exposed rock entails some scrambling, but the top of the subsidiary 3000-er called, inexplicably, Juego Bolos (Ball Game) is gained with no great difficulty.

From this simple conical summit, Caldera is revealed in all its glory. An arched fin of shattered rock with a pronounced notch in its summit, it would be seen as a giant if it were not for the massive bulk of Mulhacén towering to its left.

The linking ridge begins distinctly, but gradually subsides into the craggy escarpment, leaving the final climb as a loose and stony ramp. Once on the main ridge, turn right to traverse glinting slabs of schist to the narrow summit.

Those who are still brimming with animal strength may be

interested to know that Mulhacén's summit could be reached in a further hour of hard labour up the west flank. Lesser mortals will be more likely to sit awhile on Caldera's delectable top and observe the cabras montes (ibex) which often frequent this section of ridge.

ROUTE 19. TO LAGUNA LARGA AND CRESTONES DE RIO SECO FROM CUEVA SECRETA

Figures: 10km/1380m (to Collado de Valdeinfiernos and back)

As mentioned above, the Cueva Secreta is situated close to the foot of the valley of the Rio Valdeinfiernos. Although the most popular route from here is to Mulhacén via the Rio Valdecasillas, the Valdeinfiernos barranco provides a worthwhile ascent to its head in the wild amphitheatre of the Corral de Valdeinfiernos. This corral is comparable with the Hoya del Mulhacén, having a tremendous skyline of looming peaks in Puntal de la Caldera, Crestones de Rio Seco, and the magnificent buttress of Los Machos.

The Loma del Lanchar, with its shattered crags and the pronounced col of the Veta Grande, bounds the west side of the corral, while the Loma de Casillas (Route 18) sweeps up to the twin peaks of Juego Bolos and Puntal de la Caldera on the eastern skyline.

Nestling in a shallow hollow is the Laguna Larga (Long Tarn) which is not as pleasing to look at as Mulhacén's less attractively named Laguna de la Mosca (Tarn of the Fly), but which is just as popular as a summer camping spot.

To reach the corral from Cueva Secreta, it is simply a matter of following the 'valley of hell' as it ascends fairly easily towards the obvious serrated skyline presented by the Crestones de Rio Seco. The path is sketchy in places, but the route is straightforward and the small volume of the river makes swapping from bank to bank a simple exercise. The scenery as the corral is approached is rather reminiscent of some parts of the Cuillin of Skye, but the likely blue sky and hot sun are rather more of a rarity on the 'misty isle'.

Ascending from the Cueva, the valley proceeds on a roughly straight course until just above 1900m then makes a slight right-left kink before straightening out again. Just beyond here the Barranco

Malo enters from the right. This barranco, along with the continuing valley of the Valdeinfiernos, bounds the well defined ridge of the Arista de los Cuernos, which affords a worthwhile route onto the broad col known as the Veta Grande. Unfortunately, the Veta Grande offers no continuation for walkers onto the upper reaches of the Loma del Lanchar, the ridge being barred by repulsively shattered crags, but the situation of the col itself is well worth the effort, and those who don't mind a rough scree descent could make a crossing into the Corral del Veleta (Guarnón valley).

Continuing up the Valdeinfiernos, the Chorreras Juego de Bolos next joins from the left. This often dry side-valley rises steeply towards the col between Juego Bolos' summit and Puntal de la Caldera. It is too rough and steep to be worthwhile as an ascent route. Better to continue following the main valley as it veers slightly rightwards, heading for the impressive buttress of Los Machos. Eventually, at about 2800m above sea level, the slope eases off into the shallow Corral de Valdeinfiernos.

From here, the determined masochist can continue up a steep, loose, rough path to emerge on the main ridge at the Collado de Valdeinfiernos - a tiny notch in the Crestones de Rio Seco. Beware of cars as you emerge through the gap, though. The South Sierra Nevada Road runs within a couple of metres of the crest at this point, and it would be a shame to survive the ascent only to be the victim of a 'road accident'.

Those who expected to see the Laguna Larga in the Corral de Valdeinfiernos will be disappointed. It actually lies hidden behind a projecting spur, which bounds the eastern side of the corral itself. To reach it, traverse around the spur, keeping to the same height. There are evidences of a path, but these may prove elusive. After rounding the broad front of the spur, the Laguna will be revealed, lying like a huge puddle in a broad and flat-bottomed basin (2786m) with the usual patches of bright green turf contrasting with the arid grey slopes and crags all around.

From here, it is possible to ascend by various routes onto Puntal de la Caldera, or to traverse further east to Juego Bolos for a possible descent via the Loma de las Casillas.

ROUTE 20. TO CORRAL DEL VELETA FROM CORTIJO DE LA ESTRELLA

Figures: 13km/1600m (To Glaciar del Veleta and back)

The Guarnón barranco is a long, almost straight trench, rising directly towards the imposing north wall of Veleta. As an approach to the Corral del Veleta it is direct, but strenuous. However, it is a worthwhile route, the Guarnón having a number of picturesque waterfalls and cascades, and the crags called Tajos del Campanario gradually assume an awesome scale on the right as the Corral is approached.

From the old Cortijo buildings, begin climbing on the right bank of the river, changing to the left after 30min or so when a small irrigation channel branches from the river bed. Before long, the picturesque crag and waterfall of Chorreras Negras are reached. The crag presents a formidable obstacle, but a series of sloping shelves or 'vasares' allow walkers surprisingly easy passage to the steep slopes above.

The waterfalls are at their best in spring, when the normally small volume of water is augmented by the melting of the winter snows.

Continuing upward, the gradient shows no sign of letting up, and it is not until above the tree line (c.2500m) that there is any respite from the relentless climbing. From this point the valley broadens out, and the river splits into a number of small tributaries, draining the vast walls of the Veleta/Los Machos basin.

The terrain now assumes the characteristics of the high Sierra Nevada; barren slopes of loose stones, metallic grey slabs of schist, and areas of bright green moss wherever water is flowing. To the left, a massive scree slope with an uncomfortable path leads up to the Veta Grande saddle on the crest of the Loma del Lanchar while ahead, Veleta begins to look like the major 3000m peak it is. The Pared Norte (North Wall) with its gullies, or 'canutos' perpetually picked out in white snow is very impressive. Forming the skyline of the corral are the peaks of Los Machos, Zacatín, Campanario, Salón, and Veleta itself.

The final pull up into the Corral is a long hard slog. It is easy to fool yourself that Veleta is a lot closer that it actually is, but realisation of the Pared Norte's true stature dawns on you as you toil up this wide and barren slope.

When almost up into the Corral itself, note the mouth of the Tunel del Veleta on your right. This tunnel, now used as a rather damp and squalid bivouac, was part of a scheme which proposed to tunnel through the ridge to emerge above the ski-resort, and to bring a road through into the Corral del Veleta where a large car park would be built. Thankfully, the project was abandoned - the stark grandeur of the place would have been ruined.

The Corral is an eerily quiet and broody place, with huge piles of glacial debris, and the massive crags of Veleta looming overhead. Up to 100 years ago this corral contained the most southerly glacier in Europe, but now all that remains of the Glaciar del Veleta in the summer is a small snowfield and a tiny glacial pool at its foot. Passing by this pool is an old path which contours across the corral towards the crags of the Lanchar ridge (see Route 23).

OTHER POSSIBLE ROUTES IN THE VALLE DEL GENIL

Looking at the map of this area, a number of seemingly obvious routes stand out. The ridges, or lomas, descending from the main ridge to the valley would all appear to be straightforward climbs, leading directly from the valley bed to the high summits. However, with the exceptions of the Loma del Calvario (Route 16) and the Loma de Casillas (Route 18), they are all ruled out as walkers' routes for a number of reasons. From west to east these ridges are: the **Loma de San Juan**, which has an easy but tedious upper section, but which has no easy access from the valley bed due to private farms ('fincas') and impenetrable vegetation; the **Loma del Lanchar**, which begins promisingly from the confluence of the Rios Guarnón and Real, but encounters difficult rocks in its latter stages; the **Loma de Casillas**; and the **Loma del Calvarios**, both described above. Between these latter two ridges lies a subsidiary spur known as the Gran Espolon de Alcazaba. This is a very obvious and well known ridge, leading directly to Alcazaba's summit. It is regarded as an easy, but classic line by local climbers, but is too difficult and exposed to be recommended to the walker/scrambler.

Of the four main watercourses - San Juan, Guarnón, Valdeinfiernos, and Valdecasillas - only the San Juan barranco is ruled out. The lower part of the ravine, with the exception of the very mouth, is choked with almost Amazonian vegetation, making any attempt at an ascent totally impractical. In any case, the barranco has its head in the moderate bowl known as the Hoya de la Mora, and thus some distance from any of the main ridge summits.

It will be obvious from a perusal of the local maps that a number of possibilities exist for linking some of the above numbered routes together in 'horeseshoe' type routes. One example might include an ascent of Mulhacén via Route 17, traversing the ridge (see Routes 43, 45) to Collado del Valdeinfiernos and descending via the valley of that name back to Cueva Secreta.

See also Part 4 for Longer and Multi-Day Routes.

(B) ROUTES FROM THE SIERRA NEVADA ROAD

The Sierra Nevada Roads (RG1 to 6, RG15 and 16) provide a convenient approach to the highest summits of the range. Prior to the building of these roads all the major peaks were quite remote and were seldom climbed. The most popular route to Mulhacén in those days was the old path from Trevélez, which was the highest convenient base. Today, all that has changed. The tarmac road to Veleta brings hundreds of summer visitors to the summit daily, bringing with them all the attendant litter, noise, and even a hamburger stall at the roadhead! Even in winter, the proximity of the ski lifts brings a steady flow of people to the top. Mulhacén, too, has lost much of its old remoteness, the dirt road bringing ordinary cars to within an hour of the top, while the more adventurous driver, with a suitable vehicle, can approach to within a 10min walk of the peak via the rough Mulhacén summit road. Of the 'big three', only Alcazaba retains a certain air of impregnability, its position (on the opposite side of Mulhacén from the roads) allowing it to hide away from summer motorists and winter skiers.

However, what the roads have done for us is to provide a wealth of starting points for handy day walks. Even Alcazaba can be bagged in a few hours' walk from a car parked on the Sierra Nevada South Road.

For the purposes of this section, the term 'Sierra Nevada Road' means the entire route from Granada to Capileira including the branches to Prado Llano, Borreguiles, Las Yeguas, and Mulhacén summit.

ROUTE 21. TO PUNTAL DE LA CAZOLETA FROM PARADOR NACIONAL

Figures: 7km/330m (there and back)

The Parador is situated near to the distinctive triple summits of the Peñones de San Francisco, and is part of a small group of buildings clustered along the roadside at 2500m, overlooking the main ski

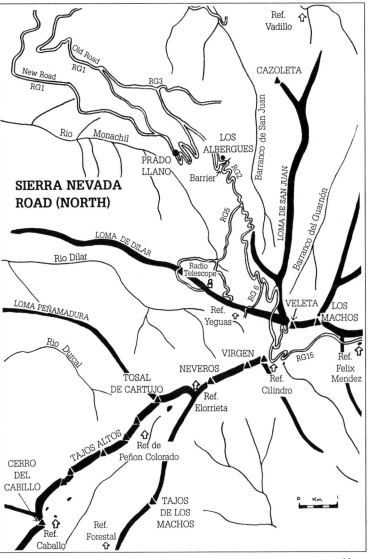

complex. The neighbouring buildings are the Albergue Universitario, a hostel owned by the University of Granada, and the Albergue de la Hoya de la Mora, a distinctive dome-roofed military hut which always seems to be shuttered and empty. Also in this vicinity are the observatory atop the Mojón del Trigo, and the statue of the Virgen de las Nieves (Virgin of the Snows).

During times of snow cover this is as far as the tarmac road goes and on sunny weekends the whole area is thronged with ski and sledge hire kiosks, hamburger stalls, and families sledging with their children. However, parking is never a problem. There are three roadside parking areas and the verges are broad and usually fairly snow-free. This area, often referred to as 'Los Albergues, makes a convenient starting point for a number of routes.

The seemingly insignificant peak of Puntal de la Cazoleta (also known as La Morra) forms a headland overlooking the Genil valley and interrupts the steady descent of the Loma de San Juan, falling from the summit of Veleta to the valley. At just over 2200m, it is actually lower than the Parador thus making this route a rather odd one - most of the climbing being done on the return. However, the summit of the Puntal is worth visiting for its views, and the walk to and from it has a number of attractions including a picturesque little waterfall in the upper Barranco de San Juan.

From the Parador, walk up the road to the Albergue Hoya de la Mora. Beside the hut is a small parking area overlooking the broad slopes of the Hoya. At the far side of this car park descend on a small path, crossing a band of low crags, then make a bee-line across light-coloured screes, heading for a small cemented cairn overlooking the upper San Juan Barranco.

Arriving at the cairn, the depth of the ravine comes as quite a surprise, being unsuspected when looking across from the Albergue. The descent to the stream is a steep, rough 200m (which has to be climbed on the return) and there may be some doubt as to which is the best route down. There are two shallow couloirs - not worth calling gullies - one on each side of the cairn. The right-hand one looks more obvious, but is rougher. Better to start towards the left side of the left-hand couloir, where the prickly vegetation is a bit more sparse and the scree a little less loose.

Keeping to the left all the way down, descend this unpleasant slope until a small path appears, leading down the side of a large slab to reach the stream bed by the side of a lovely little waterfall. This a great place for a cooling rest on a hot day, prior to starting across the sunny slope of the Loma de San Juan.

The route from here follows the line of an old irrigation channel, or 'acequia', which departs from the stream bed just below the waterfall to traverse along the 2200m contour to the col behind the summit of Puntal de la Cazoleta. These old channels, quite common in the Sierra Nevada, are remarkable feats of primitive agricultural engineering, often traversing long stretches of rough terrain while maintaining the slight descent necessary for flow. The acequia which leads to Puntal de la Cazoleta now carries water only in its early stages, but its course continues as an obvious path, descending so slightly that it is almost imperceptible.

On reaching the shallow col behind the peak, it is a simple matter to ascend the short slope leading to the summit. The views of the Genil valley from here are superb, Güéjar Sierra being particularly well seen, along with the whole length of the upper valley's deeply incised trench leading via the various tributaries to the towering north walls with their corrals and hoyas. A rather less pleasing sight is the Albergue above the Hoya de la Mora, which now appears to be much higher than expected on the edge of the Peñones de San Francisco ridge. It is no illusion. The Albergue is 300m higher, and the return leg is rather harder than anticipated. Any ascent encountered after bagging your main objective is always resented, but there is an alternative described below.

ROUTE 22. THE ASCENT OF VELETA VIA PUNTAL DE LA CAZOLETA AND LOMA DE SAN JUAN, RETURNING VIA THE NORTH WEST RIDGE. FROM PARADOR NACIONAL

Figures: 15km/1220m

The route to the summit of Puntal de la Cazoleta is described above, but the uphill return leg is avoided by making Veleta the ultimate objective. This produces a much tougher outing altogether, but a more aesthetically pleasing circular one, with a proper mountain

Corral del Veleta from Loma de San Juan

ridge-walk to the top and an easy final downhill walk back to the Parador.

Follow Route 21 to reach the crest of the Loma de San Juan, then turn right to ascend the ridge towards the summit. The ridge is initially broad and grassy, and climbs in three stages, passing over the minor headlands of Atalayón Chico (c.2375m) and Atalayón Grande (c.2425m) with flatter sections in between. The views improve steadily as height is gained and the character of the ridge itself gradually changes, becoming narrower and more stony. By the time the 2500m level is reached (level with the Albergues) the Loma is a well defined ridge, with occasional bare rock to add interest to the ascent. The walking remains easy, but the unacclimatised will by now be feeling the slight breathlessness of altitude.

As the 2800m contour is crossed, the slope on the left, dropping into the Guarnón valley, becomes a line of crags (Tajos del Campanario) and the views over the edge of these crags into the Corral del Veleta become more and more breathtaking as height is gained. The ridge is now turning into a real mountain arête, especially in winter when crampons and ice axe are essential. In summer, the ratio of living rock to loose stones is swinging in favour of bare slabs of shiny schist.

At 3100m, any illusions of Himalayan mountaineering are suddenly shattered when the Sierra Nevada Road is encountered. A couple of small ruined buildings stand atop the ridge here, and just beyond, for a few metres you must share the crest with hire cars from Málaga. Luckily, the road soon opts for a rising traverse across the western slopes of the ridge, and you can continue up the slabs and boulders which form the ridge crest hereabouts. Note that the path to the bed of the Corral del Veleta via the Veredon Superior departs from the road at this point (see Route 23).

Now the ridge rears up purposefully towards the peak, and some excellent slabs and blocks provide a little scrambling on this final approach to the summit. In winter, this section can contain a lot of ice, and it is worth treating with caution under those conditions. At any time outside the months of July and August, snowfields may be encountered and snow at this altitude will be very hard. An ice axe may be an invaluable aid to cut steps safely across any large patches.

Zacatin, Campanario, Salón and Veleta from the head of the Veredon Superior

The ridge terminates abruptly in a sharp prow at the summit of Veleta, and the peak would be a first class mountain top were it not for the ugly concrete building, the graffiti-daubed survey post, the roadhead, the blazed path from the road up the final few metres, and the ubiquitous litter. This is one summit which is best visited in the grip of a severe winter, when much of the man-made clutter is hidden under snow.

The view is also better in winter, when there is less haze and the coast of Africa may be seen over the coastal range and the expanse of the Mediterranean Sea. The rugged grandeur of the main ridge, stretching away to the east and the south-west, is impressive at any time of year, as is the huge drop into the Corral del Veleta.

To return to the Parador, retrace your steps along the ridge (no hardship as this is an excellent arête) as far as the road bend and small ruin at 3100m. This is the point at which the Loma de San Juan and the North West Ridge separate, forming two 'arms' which embrace the Hoya de la Mora and the San Juan Barranco. Take the less distinct ridge on the left, which carries the road, and head for the distinct landmarks of the Mojon del Trigo observatory, and the Virgen de las Nieves. In bad visibility, the line is initially north-west,

Looking up the Veredon Superior. Photo by Ian Roberts

but the road is a good landmark, much of its track being discernible even during winter. After leaving the Loma de San Juan at the 3100m bend, you will touch the road at two more hairpin bends, then follow the ridge over a more distinct, rocky section before rejoining the road as it zig-zags down the final broad ridge to the Mojon del Trigo, and the zone of Los Albergues. Easy walking, shortcutting the road's tortuous route, brings you back to the Parador. This is one of the most satisfying day-routes available from the Sierra Nevada Road.

ROUTE 23. CORRAL DEL VELETA AND LOS MACHOS VIA VEREDON SUPERIOR

Figures: 4km/425m (including return)

There is one point on the Veleta summit road where the road touches the actual crest of the north ridge (Loma de San Juan) and it is here that the path into the Corral del Veleta begins - see RG2.

The road reaches the ridge at a sharp hairpin bend just beyond k 44. Approximately 150m beyond the bend, a small one-car parking space on the left marks the beginning of the path to the Veredon Superior.

The path heads straight for the edge of the crag overlooking the Corral del Veleta, but actually leads onto a broad terrace just below the top edge. This terrace rises slightly, following below the low upper band of crag, and soon reaches a little col where the Veredon is suddenly revealed.

This remarkable feature is a perfectly simple rake, leading straight down to the floor of the corral. It cuts diagonally across the face of the vertical Tajos del Campanario, and affords the only easy way for walkers to reach the corral from the Sierra Nevada Road. Note that in winter, huge cornices form on the edge of the Tajos, and the Veredon is graded 'Dificil' as a winter climb. It doesn't tend to hold snow beyond May, however, so in the June to September period it should present no problems.

Descend the Veredon on a perfectly simple path which arrives on the corral floor amid piles of loose rock and ibex droppings. The path continues, quite distinct, and crosses the 'mouth' of the corral, passing the remnants of the Veleta 'glacier' with its cold green pool and heading purposefully towards the Lanchar ridge. It appears to be heading towards the Paso de las Monteses, a col below the upper crags of Los Machos, but the traverse below the crags, and a stone footbridge across a gully, have been obliterated by a massive rockfall. The whole crag-face in this area looks very unstable, and it is definitely a place to avoid.

To reach the summit of Los Machos, leave the path just beyond the glacial pool and climb along the crest of a series of glacial moraines. These lead onto a rather unpleasant slope of scree and boulders, but this eventually eases off onto the broad saddle between the jagged ridge of Veleta/Salón/Campanario/Zacatín, and Los Machos. The summit is reached across a wide stony whaleback.

Veleta and the Guarón valley from Cortijo de la Estrella

View from Mulhacén summit car park over Caldera, Loma Pela and Rio
Seco to Los Machos and Veleta

Alcazaba and Mulhacén from Loma de San Juan

ROUTE 24. TO THE ELORRIETA HUT FROM THE YEGUAS HUT

Figures: 3.5km/270m (excluding return)

The Refugio de las Yeguas can be reached by the dirt road (RG6) which leaves the Sierra Nevada Road at about 3050m. Alternatively, it is possible to drive to the radio telescope on the crest of the Loma de Dilar, reached via the Borreguiles road (RG5), and walk from there along the ridge to the Dilar observatory, from which point the Yeguas hut is seen below and easily reached by descending a rough 4WD track which links up with the Yeguas access track. There is plenty of parking space near both the radio telescope and the Refugio de las Yeguas.

From the hut, skirt the embankment of the Yeguas reservoir on its east side and pick up a small path climbing southwards to a higher shelf which contains the Lagunillas de la Virgen - a line of either small pools or snow patches, depending on the time of year. The path improves as the Lagunillas are passed and soon joins a broad and well engineered path. This path, which originates at the Veleta col on the main ridge, is actually much used on the Integral de los Tres Mil (Route 45) as a detour avoiding the craggy section of ridge over Tajos del Neveros and Tajos de la Virgen (Route 25).

On reaching the main path, turn right and follow it as it climbs in zig-zags through a chaos of huge boulders. Causeways carry the path over the worst sections as it skirts high across a shallow corrie, with the curious gendarme known as El Fraile de Capileira visible on the skyline. At the far side of this corrie, the path climbs more steeply for a while, but soon emerges on the broad shoulder of the Elorrieta ridge, with the hut just beyond.

The Refugio de Elorrieta (wrongly marked on IGN map) occupies a tremendous position on the very crest of the main ridge at 3150m. It stands at the head of the Lanjarón valley, at the bifurcation of the main ridge. Straight ahead, the ridge of Tajos de los Machos bounds the south-eastern side of the valley, while branching off rightwards is the long craggy ridge over Tosal de Cartujo and Tajos Altos, bounding the north-western side and culminating in the domed summit of Cerro del Caballo - the most westerly 3000-er. The hut is built partially underground, and is now mostly in ruins. It must have once been quite a well appointed place. The remnants of mozaic tiled floors inside the shell hint at more opulent times, when the hut would have been a grand place to spend the night. Nowadays, it could be a lifesaver in a blizzard, but at other times it has an almost spooky atmosphere, rather like a ghost town - once full of life, now abandoned.

The Elorrieta hut is a focal point on the ascents of Tajos de los Machos and Cerro del Caballo from the east (Routes 26 and 27).

ROUTE 25. TO ELORRIETA VIA TAJOS DE LA VIRGEN FROM COL DEL VELETA

Figures: 6km/200-300m (incl. return. depending on route choice)

The parking area at the Collado del Veleta (see RG2 and RG15) provides a convenient starting point for the traverse of the rough crest of Tajos del Neveros and Tajos de la Virgen. It is quite close to the turnaround point for the daily buses from Granada; the junction which is the only place with room for the bus to turn is just 400m up the road, so it is possible for walkers without cars to visit the western summits with relative ease.

The ridge between the Collado del Veleta and the Elorrieta hut is one of the most rugged sections of the main ridge and, despite little distance and climb, it is very time-consuming. There are many small summits, and various names are applied to them. The distinctive pinnacle known as El Fraile de Capileira is a prominent landmark about halfway along the ridge, and can be seen from a long way away, especially when picked out by snow. El Fraile (The Friar) is so named because of its resemblance to a priest with a long cloak when seen from the vicinity of las Yeguas. The two main summits on the ridge are known as Tajos de la Virgen and Tajos del Neveros.

Starting from the parking area, a broad path leads off in the direction of the first crags. This path bypasses an initial hump on the north side to reach the ridge crest in 100m. From here the crest can be followed over two pinnacles by those with scrambling ability and a good head for heights, but others will follow the normal route, which crosses the ridge to descend slightly across the south side to a shoulder. Now the path fizzles out but scree slopes can be crossed to rejoin the crest below the crags of the main summit. A direct ascent is obviously out of the question, but by crossing back to the north side an easy ascent on good clean slabs and blocks can be made to reach the summit with its slender cairn.

Easy walking, keeping slightly on the northern side, now leads down to a sandy col just before El Fraile. Skirting the base of the pinnacle to the south side brings you to the most awkward section. The crest is now out of the question, being composed of massive splintered rocks, and a way must be found over a chaos of big blocks on the south side. As the craggy prow of the second main summit looms there seems to be no way ahead, but at about half height on the southern crags you will find a sloping terrace which leads directly across the face, with small ups and downs, to emerge on a loose rocky slope which leads up to the crest just beyond the top. A short backtrack along the broad slabby ridge brings you to the actual summit.

The Elorrieta hut is now just a short walk away, and is not seen until it is actually underfoot - most of the building being underground.

ROUTE 26. TO TAJOS DE LOS MACHOS FROM ELORRIETA HUT

Figures: 6km/200m (including return)

The fairly unremarkable peak of Tajos de los Machos is worth a visit mainly for its excellent views. The walk can be started from either the Refugio de las Yeguas, or the Collado del Veleta, the routes from those places to the Refugio de Elorrieta being described above.

From Elorrieta, do not be tempted to follow the distinct path just below the crest on the north-west side. This leads into a zig-zag descent which would take you down into the Lanjarón valley and onto the Vereda Cortada (see Route 27).

Follow the crest of the ridge as it heads south-west, passing the heads of a number of gullies with spectacular views down into the valleys of the Alpujarras. The ridge is rough underfoot, but affords quite easy walking for the most part. After the initial mild descent from the hut, the ridge begins climbing only very slightly, leading up gradually to a short rocky rise, after which the ridge smooths out again, and the summit is brought underfoot after a final easy uphill walk.

The view across the Lanjarón valley to the long switchback of Tajos Altos and Cerro del Caballo is superb, as is the wide panorama over the southern slopes of the Sierra Nevada and the Alpujarras, the surprising length of the Loma del Mulhacén being especially well seen from this vantage point.

ROUTE 27. TO CERRO DEL CABALLO FROM ELORRIETA HUT. OUTWARD VIA TAJOS ALTOS, RETURNING VIA THE VEREDA CORTADA

Figures: 14km/650m

As is the case with Route 26 above, this walk can be started from either the Yeguas hut, or the Veleta col. However, the traverse of the Tajos Altos ridge is very rough and takes longer than you might image. Also, the majority of the route is above 3000m and the fatiguing effects of the altitude should not be underestimated. Unless very fit and well acclimatised, it's a good idea to start early and allow plenty of time for the completion of this route.

From the Elorrieta hut, descend stony slopes northwards to cross a wide hollow at the head of the Lanjarón valley. If coming from the Yeguas hut it is possible to turn off the path before reaching the Elorrieta hut and cross the hollow in a more westerly direction. A curious feature in this depression is a large square patch in the stones. This patch is much too big to be a helipad and I have been unable to discover its purpose.

At the far side of the depression, work up a rocky slope (obstacles easily avoided) and gain the ridge a short distance from the top of Tosal de Cartujo. The summit of this peak is formed of a curious outcrop of huge blocks of stone, which the cabra montes (ibex) has no trouble surmounting, but which may give humans a certain amount of trouble. Descending northwards from the summit is a celebrated ridge called the Arista del Cartujo. This is graded 'Muy Dificil' (very difficult) as a winter climb, and is therefore outside the scope of this book, but it is worth looking out for. It is well seen from the vicinity of El Fraile de Capileira.

The ridge of Tajos Altos leaves the summit in a south-westerly direction, and is a rough traverse with many ups and downs and no relief from the sharp, stony terrain underfoot. The views make it worthwhile, however, and this is one of the best ridges in the Sierra Nevada on which to observe the ibex at close quarters.

A succession of rocky summits, gradually declining in height, leads eventually to the wide col below Cerro del Caballo. From here, a small path leads up the final 100m of ascent to the summit. This is a fine headland, the last peak of the range before its long descent to the valley of the Rio Guadalfeo. The summit itself is adorned with a concrete survey post, a rain gauge, and large quantities of goat droppings - this is obviously a favourite haunt of the ibex; perhaps they appreciate the view. Humans certainly should, for it encompasses a wide vista over the greens of the western Alpujarras, the browns of the Contraviesa coastal hills, and beyond, the blue of the Mediterranean Sea. To the west, you look down across the vast bowl of the Torrente corrie, while to the east and north-east lie the profound depths of the Lanjarón valley, and the enclosed hanging valley of the Laguna del Caballo. It is a superb panorama.

An easier return to the Elorrieta hut is provided by the excellent path known as the Vereda Cortada. Its name, meaning 'the cut path', should not be allowed to put you off unduly. The 'cut' referred to is a steep gully, which scythes through the path as it traverses along a craggy face. The stride across the gap is aided by a sturdy chain, and will cause difficulty only to the most nervous of walkers.

Leave the summit of Caballo by retracing your upward steps to the col at 2909m (north of the peak). From here, a steep and loose path leads down to the brooding Laguna del Caballo, with the Refugio del Caballo on its eastern shore. The Refugio is a quaint little building with a curved roof and a chimney stack, and its interior is less squalid than many of the Sierra Nevada's bivouac

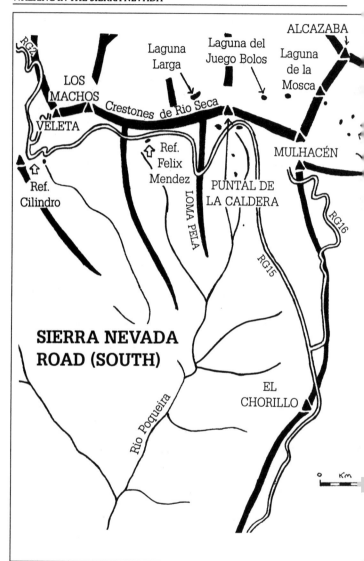

LAGUNAS

Río Culo Perro

Río Trevélez

TREVÉLEZ

RG12

shelters, but it is gloomy, and provides only the most basic of shelter. In good weather I'm sure most people would prefer to spend the night in a tent on the grassy sward alongside rather than in the damp confines of the hut.

Running past the hut door, a few metres away, is a good path. Rightwards (SSW) the path leads to the ruins of the Ventura hut, en route to Lanjarón, while to the left (NNE) it leads via the crags of Tajos Altos to the Elorrieta hut. It is this section which is called the Vereda Cortada.

This path must have been painstakingly engineered originally. It has long stretches of causeway to carry it over the frequent stream beds and boulder fields (though some have begun to collapse), and its route is ingenious in searching out the line of least resistance across a long stretch of very rugged mountainside. It winds its way along, rising and falling at easy gradients, and passes the often dry bed of the Laguna Cuadrada. The rock scenery of the chaotic faces of Tajos Altos along here is spectacular.

After about 30 to 40min easy walking, the path can no longer find an easy route at this level and suddenly makes a short, steep zig-zag ascent to reach a high terrace crossing the face of a big crag. The path levels off again and, remaining broad and easy, begins to traverse across the face. The 'paso malo' (bad passage) is reached abruptly on rounding a bend in the path. A steep gully approximately 1.5m wide cuts through the shelf which carries the path. The bed of the gully is smooth, but has been fitted with a thick chain to provide security while you make the long stride, or jump, across the gap. Safely on the other side,

103

continue along the terrace to a sudden sharp descent, which takes the path back down to easier ground.

Long stretches of easy causeway and man-made rock steps take the path into the head of the Lanjarón valley, passing the small pool of Laguna Bolaños en route. Below the path on the right as you approach the valley head lies the Refugio de Peñon Colorado, which translates as the 'refuge of the colourful rock outcrop'. It is aptly named because the refuge consists of a natural mass of rocks into which the building has been incorporated - a sort of semi man-made shelter. Sadly, like almost all the Sierra Nevada's once impressive list of huts, this one too has fallen into disrepair.

If you have been observing the Elorrieta hut, high on its ridge, as you came along the path, you will by now have realised that a fair bit of climbing is yet required to reach it. Over 200m of it in fact. The path loops across the valley, crossing the infant Rio Lanjarón, and reaches a T-junction with another path. Turn left (to the right, the path heads off across the eastern slopes of the valley, to rendezvous with the Rio Chico valley track - RG14) and commence the long drag up to the Elorrieta hut. The path climbs in long zig-zags until almost up to the ridge, then makes a bee-line for the hut. Gradients are relatively easy, but at this stage of the day, and at this altitude girding up of loins will be required.

ROUTE 28. ASCENT OF LOS MACHOS FROM FELIX MENDEZ HUT

Figures: 5km/300m (including return)

The Refugio de Felix Mendez is by far the best known, best equipped, and best maintained of the Sierra Nevada's mountain huts. Owned by the FEM, the hut has a main building with 50 bunks, a radio telephone and a warden in residence during summer, and also a smaller extension which serves as a bivouac shelter during the months when the main building is closed. There is an agreement with the Union of International Alpine Associations, so it is possible for members of affiliated organisations to book accommodation via their own clubs etc.

The hut is situated at 3040m, in the broad, flat bottomed Rio Seco corrie, among the group of uninspiring pools known as the Lagunas de Rio Seco. The ridges enclosing this corre are anything but uninspiring, however. To the west, the viciously jagged arête of the Raspones de Rio Seco ('raspón' = a cut or graze), which is reminiscent of the Chamonix Aguilles on a much smaller scale, plunges down towards the Poqueira ravine. Bounding the eastern side is the huge but featureless ridge of Loma Pelada (Peeled Ridge), while forming the northern skyline is the pinnacled main ridge, the Crestones de Rio Seco, with the South Sierra Nevada Road clinging to its flank (see RG15).

The hut, or the limited parking space on the road opposite the hut access track, makes a convenient starting point for a number of walks. As well as Los Machos, ascents of Loma Pelada, Puntal de la Caldera, Juego de Bolos, Mulhacén or even Alcazaba can be made in day trips from the hut.

Los Machos is the nearest major peak to the Felix Mendez hut, and to reach its summit is a relatively simple matter. Leave the hut along the access track which leads up to the road, and follow the road westward. Pass through the notch cut through the Raspones de Rio Seco ridge and continue easily along the stony track, which keeps very close to the ridge crest hereabouts. The ridge itself is composed of a series of pinnacles and narrow cols (excellent views into the Valdeinfiernos corrie) and it is obviously impractical to attempt to traverse the crest. Shortly you will reach the Collado de Valdeinfiernos (sometimes called the Collado del Ciervo - Col of the Stag) where the path from the Valdeinfiernos valley emerges. The col is a narrow gap right by the road.

From here, the ridge sweeps up into the bulk of Los Machos, and the road escapes by veering left to traverse across a vast scree slope. No such evasion for walkers aiming for the summit, though. The only way up is to tackle the scree, an unpleasant task, but the summit is worth it.

Small paths will be seen in the scree, but no path survives for long on this slope, and their routes are constantly altering.

Head for a fairly prominent gully cutting through a band of rock high up the face; this is the gateway to the top. Upon reaching this gully, clamber up easy rock steps to emerge on the upper slopes, with the summit just a few metres' easy walk away. The top itself is a broad rocky dome with a memorial tablet, and a rusty metal box which must have once contained a 'visitor's book'. The views are tremendous, especially down the Guarnón valley to the Genil, and Mulhacén and Alcazaba are also well seen from here. It will be obvious that 'nipping across to bag Veleta' is out of the question; the ridge between the two peaks switchbacks over the jagged 'fangs' of Zacatin, Campanario, and Salón, and ends in a vertical cliff below Veleta's summit. However, it is an interesting little diversion to explore this ridge as far as courage and ability allow. The exposed summits of the 'fangs' make thrilling viewpoints, but beware of loose rocks - the fissured schist composing this ridge is notoriously unreliable.

ROUTE 29. LOMA PELA AND PUNTAL DE LA CALDERA FROM FELIX MENDEZ HUT

Figures: 6.5km/370m (incl. return via Laguna and road)

The broad and rather featureless ridge of Loma Pela actually forms one of the range's 3000-ers though it is seldom, if ever, climbed for its own sake. It is a major obstacle across your path if you are heading from the hut to the far worthier peak of Puntal de la Caldera. The Sierra Nevada Road also finds it a formidable barrier and makes a long loop to the south to circumvent the difficulty.

However, if aiming for Puntal de la Caldera from the Felix Mendez or anywhere west of Loma Pela, then it is as easy to traverse the summit of the ridge as to circumvent it by following the road.

From the hut, climb up to the road along the access track and follow it as it heads east below the jagged Crestones de Rio Seco. The Crestones are a prominent main ridge feature, but traversing the tops of the multiple pinnacles is a totally impractical notion. For a distance of 1.5km - from Collado de Valdeinfiernos to Loma Pela - the crest of the main ridge is a long succession of sharp-edged pinnacles and narrow gaps and the road, which runs close by, is invariably used to avoid what would be a difficult and time-consuming traverse.

Rio Seco corral and Felix Mendez hut from Loma Pela

As the bulky hump of Loma Pela is approached, the road swings south along the flank of the ridge. From here, a small path will be seen climbing the easy, but stony, slope ahead. This path will take you to the top of the ridge, which is a broad whaleback carpeted with small schisty stones. The ridge has two summits (merely slight rises on the plateau), the highest - by one metre - being the more southerly one at 3188m. The northerly one has by far the best views, however, being positioned at the edge of the northern escarpment overlooking the upper Valdeinfierno and the corrie of Laguna Larga.

Puntal de la Caldera is now in full view, rising craggily across the deep caldron in which lies the circular Laguna de la Caldera. It is easy to see how the name was inspired, the laguna and its jagged rim being very reminiscent of an extinct volcano crater.

Unfortunately, the ridge crest leading to the summit is out of bounds for walkers, having a huge notch which demands unpleasant moves on shattered and unreliable rock on its western side, and which has a vertical cliff forming its eastern wall. However, a small path traverses diagonally from the shallow col between Loma

Pela's two tops to gain access to the bottom of this notch after crossing steep slabs covered with loose stones and gravel - care necessary! Once in the notch, cross to the northern side of the ridge and then gain the summit via a system of steps and ledges on that side. There are a number of possible routes, none of them difficult, but made unpleasant by the quantity of loose stones. The summit is a tilted slab of refreshingly clean rock with superb views all around.

To avoid retracing steps, leave the summit eastwards towards the Collado del Mulhacén (also sometimes called the Collado del Ciervo or the Collado de la Mosca) and then descend over boulder slopes to the parking area by the side of the Laguna de la Caldera, a popular stopping place for summer motorists, and the starting point for the easiest way up Mulhacén (Route 30). From here, it is possible to climb back over Loma Pela or to follow the road as it loops around the ridge. If the road is quiet (i.e. if it is not a weekend in July or August) then it makes for an easy return with good views to the south. On busy weekends, the dust from passing vehicles can make it unpleasant.

ROUTE 30. THE ASCENT OF MULHACÉN FROM CALDERA PARKING

Figures: 3km/445m (direct ascent and descent)
Possibly MBF

Parking by the roadside is easy either next to the Laguna de la Caldera or near to the smaller - sometimes dry - Laguna de la Caldereta a little further along the road. It will be obvious that this route could also be used by parties based at the Felix Mendez hut - possibly combined with Route 29 above. Mulhacén's wide and featureless west face provides an easy ascent to the summit in less than an hour, with almost limitless route choice. Keeping close to the ridge gives spectacular views down into the Hoya del Mulhacén.

Actually, this is not **the** easiest way to the top. The Mulhacén summit road (RG16) approaches within 800m (10min) of the top, but unless in possession of a 4WD type vehicle most people will consider this rough road an unjustifiable abuse of the car. Mountain bikers, on the other hand, may well regard this as a good opportunity to ride to the highest summit in Spain, and the west face is probably a bikeable descent to a confident and experienced mountain biker. The loop from Caldera to the top via the road, with a descent of the west face, would make an excellent bike outing.

For those on foot, a better expedition is provided by climbing to the Collado del Mulhacén and descending on a distinct path into the Hoya del Mulhacén, then traversing the peak via El Corredor, the north-east ridge and a descent of the west face. This route is described as part of Route 17 from the Genil valley.

ROUTE 31. THE ASCENT OF ALCAZABA FROM CALDERA PÁRKING

Figures: 8km/925m (there and back via El Corredor)

Although the lowest of the 'big three' peaks (Mulhacén, Veleta and Alcazaba), Alcazaba (The Citadel) is the most rugged. It has the most challenging name, the grandest outline, and the most difficult access. The aloofness of Alcazaba, completely unsullied by roads or tracks, is maintained partly by its impressive battlements - crags surround it on three sides - and partly by its remote position - hiding behind its obese brother, Mulhacén. Compared with 'big brother', Alcazaba is a ruffian; uncouth in apearance and unfriendly to strangers, it attracts relatively few visitors, but those who make the effort to approach it and find a way through its forbidding walls will come to regard Alcazaba as the true king peak of the Sierra Nevada.

In winter, Alcazaba is a peak of alpine character. All approaches are arduous and all except the long east and south-east ridges contain graded mountaineering difficulties.

During the summer, though, the peak relents and allows access to mere adventurous walkers, who can reach its summit most easily from the South Sierra Nevada Road via the Hoya del Mulhacén and El Corredor.

From the Caldera/Caldereta parking, climb up to the Collado del Mulhacén and descend the small path into the Hoya del Mulhacén. The scree covered ramps of El Corredor (see Route 17) can now be used to gain the main ridge between Mulhacén and Puntal de Siete Lagunas. This route is much easier than traversing Mulhacén. Turn left and walk up easy steps to the summit of the insignificant Puntal, from where a daunting view of Alcazaba's south-western crags ('tajos') is obtained.

It is palpably obvious from this viewpoint that a direct traverse of the ridge to the summit is out of the question. A big step bars the way, mirroring the situation on the opposite side of the mountain. Luckily, the crags on this side are not as continuous as the overhanging Tajos del Goteron, and a way can be found through them by traversing rightwards to a broad scree fan which allows access to the upper slopes. The scree fan is steep and as unpleasant as only Sierra Nevada scree can be, but there is no technical difficulty, and you will eventually emerge on the bouldery terrain above. The best way to the summit is to keep to the edge of the escarpment and enjoy the superb views as you traverse the ridge to the peaked top.

There is no obvious alternative return route, but if the intention is to bag Mulhacén **and** Alcazaba, then the best plan is to traverse Mulhacén first, returning via El Corredor and the Hoya. That way, most of the worst scree is taken in descent.

ROUTE 32. TO CAÑADA DE LAS SIETE LAGUNAS FROM MULHACÉN SUMMIT ROAD (RG16)

Figures: 6km/100m (to Laguna Hondera and back)

The Cañada de las Siete Lagunas (canyon of the seven tarns) is a well known feature on the southern side of the range. It nestles between Mulhacén and Alcazaba, and is popular as a high camping place, having a wealth of grassy pitches (hard to come by in the high Sierra Nevada) and clean running water everywhere.

The shortest way into the Cañada is either to descend into it from the top of the Mulhacén Summit Road (steep scree descent), or to traverse into it, roughly along the 2900m contour. The latter is preferable, if only because return to the vehicle is so much easier.

To find the best starting point, turn into the Mulhacén Summit

Road and follow it as it sweeps around a long left-hand bend and begins winding its way up the lower part of the Loma del Mulhacén (Loma del Tanto on IGN map). The road proceeds in easy bends until c.2930m when it encounters a sharp hairpin to the right. Park either just before or just after this bend where the road is wider (Laguna de Peñon Negro on the right).

Set out across the rocky slopes in a north-westerly direction, maintaining height as much as possible. Some slight climbing and descending is necessary to avoid craggy ground but it is possible to progress along a broad sloping shelf in the 2900m to 2950m band. Eventually, you will approach the rocky spur called the Tajo del Contadero. This spur has a flattish shoulder at just over 2950m and it becomes necessary to climb slightly to cross this shoulder and enter the Cañada de las Siete Lagunas.

The Cañada is a wide hanging valley, with a floor which rises at a gentle gradient towards the main watershed, with the little peak of Puntal de Siete Lagunas sitting atop the ridge between the bulk of Mulhacén and Alcazaba. The floor of this sloping corrie is sprinkled with small pools and laced with rushing meltwater streams. The lowest and largest of the seven tarns is named Laguna Hondera while the highest, tucked up against the headwall, is aptly christened Laguna Altera. The five smaller ones, along with other little pools, are unnamed.

This corrie is probably the best wild-camping place in the Sierra Nevada, being free of litter, comparatively secluded, grandly situated between the two most majestic peaks of the range, and abundantly provided with both fresh running water and soft grassy pitches. It is seldom without at least one tent.

See Route 35 for the longer approach to the Cañada from Trevélez.

(C) THE ALPUJARRAS AND MARQUESADO FOREST

The Alpujarra has a unique character and atmosphere - totally different from the north and western area of the range. Smooth contours, long valleys and terraced slopes are dotted with tiny whitewashed villages. The moorish influence is everywhere apparent: in the placenames, in the architecture of the villages, and in the methods of agriculture (many of which are still used). A system of narrow and tortuous roads links these villages, finally finding a way over the main ridge at the Puerto de la Ragua at the eastern end. The pass leads over to the equally attractive but again different Marquesado del Zenete pine forest at the edge of the huge Guadix plain.

The southern slopes of the Sierra Nevada are long, grassy and gentle, and are penetrated by a number of river valleys. Towards the east, these valleys become gradually shallower and less well defined, but the four most westerly penetrate deep into the heart of the 3000m zone. From the western end, these four are: the Valle del Lanjarón, the Rio Chico valley, the Barranco del Poqueira, and the Valle del Trevélez.

The Lanjarón valley is a long trench, rising as straight as an arrow from the town at 660m to the lonely Laguna de Lanjarón at almost 3000m. The lower part of the valley is sparsely wooded, and has been heavily cultivated with large areas of the valley sides being terraced and criss-crossed with old irrigation channels ('acequias'). Once a popular route of approach to Cerro del Caballo, the old paths have fallen into disfavour as a result of new access tracks on the Loma del Caballo, and the easier approach from the Sierra Nevada Road (see Route 27), and have become overgrown in places.

The upper valley is narrow and enclosed by the looming crags of Tajos Altos and the featureless slope of Tajo de los Machos. There are no paths in the valley bed, but there are routes along both valley sides, one - the Vereda Cortada - threading along the face of Tajos Altos from Caballo (Route 27). The other traverses the south-east slopes and is a non-motorable extension of the Chico valley track (RG14). Both paths rendezvous below the Laguna de Lanjarón before climbing to the Elorrieta hut at the valley head.

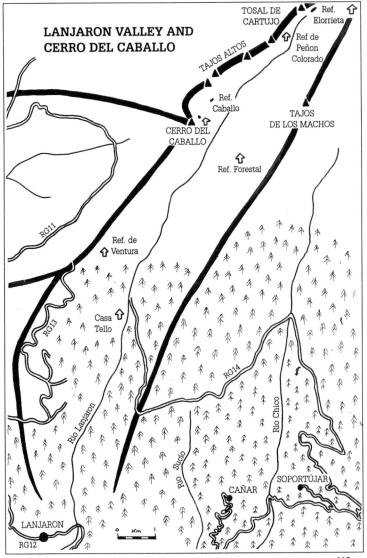

LANJARON VALLEY AND
CERRO DEL CABALLO

The Chico valley is much shorter than the Valle del Lanjarón, and drains a relatively insignificant area between the Loma de Cañar and the side spur known as the Loma Casilla de los Moros. It provides no convenient direct access to the 3000m peaks. However, the valley carries a long and tortuous dirt track (RG14) which does provide access to the upper Lanjarón valley, and ultimately to the Elorrieta hut (walkers and mountain bikers only). The valley is extensively forested and the forestry commission is very sensitive about access in the hot months. In August 1992 extensive forest fires in the Chico valley destroyed large areas, a disaster which made the national news.

The next valley eastwards is the impressive **Barranco del Poqueira**, a huge ravine whose upper tributaries penetrate far into the high zone. The streams draining away from Laguna de la Caldera (Rio Mulhacén), the Rio Seco corrie, the Laguna de Aguas Verdes (Rio Veleta) and the huge bowl below the Virgen/Elorrieta ridge (Rio Puntal) all unite in the Poqueira ravine, first as the Rio Naute, and then the Rio Poqueira. It is a profound, V-shaped valley, but much more open than the deeply incised Valle del Genil to the north of the range, having large areas of cultivated terraces on its slopes.

The showcase moorish villages of Capileira, Bubión and Pampaneira cling to the eastern slopes of the lower valley, forming a picturesque scene popular on Alpujarran postcards. Tourism is being actively encouraged hereabouts; Bubión in particular is being developed as a holiday centre. At the time of writing, all three villages retain their old world charm, but this may not remain true indefinitely. Capileira is usually regarded as the staring point of the South Sierra Nevada Road, though it really starts at Pampaneira where it has its junction with the GR421 (see RG12/RG15).

Although a glance at the map may suggest that the Poqueira and its tributaries form logical routes to the high peaks, there are no frequented ascent routes by the watercourses in this valley.

The Trevélez valley has a different character altogether. Straight and fairly narrow, the valley rises only relatively gently but eventually reaches right up to the very crest of the range at the Puerto de Trevélez (2798m). This is one of the Sierra Nevada's main foot-passes, linking Trevélez in the Alpujarras with Jeres del

Marquesado in the magnificent Marquesado del Zenete forest on the north side.

Tucked away up this valley is Trevélez itself, Spain's highest village. The GR421 road makes a long loop to climb up the west side of the valley to the village before returning down the eastern side. Trevélez, as its name suggests, is actually three villages or 'barrios' built close together, the lowest straddling the road at 1480m, while the highest buildings in Barrio Alto stand at almost 1600m. The village has an excellent campsite, which is open all year. Remember, however, that it can get very cold at this altitude in winter. I say this from personal experience!

Above the village the valley rises pleasantly among farms, irrigation channels and conifers, gradually narrowing as it approaches the crowding ridges descending from the high peaks. A prominent side-valley on the left is that of the Rio Culo de Perro (Dog's Arse River!) which drains the Cañada de las Siete Lagunas. The main valley continues, now much narrower, to a prominent fork at the foot of the southern ridge of the aptly named 3180m peak of Horcajo de Trevélez (Fork of Trevélez). To the right the Trevélez valley leads up to the high col of Puerto de Trevélez. The left-hand branch is the valley of the Rio Juntillas, draining the eastern slopes of Puntal de Vacares, El Cuervo, and La Atalaya.

Trevélez was the most popular starting point for the ascent of Mulhacén before the South Sierra Nevada Road was built in the mid 1960s. The route goes via El Chorillo, Loma del Tanto and Loma del Mulhacén, but the ridge from El Chorillo is now occupied by the road. It is still a good way to the summit in winter, though, having no difficulties and 'only' 2000m of ascent.

Surprisingly there are only two centres with good routes for walkers, and these are Lanjarón and Trevélez. All the other towns and villages are either too remote, are surrounded by cultivated land with no paths, or have good vehicular routes to the mountains (Capileira, Bubión) leaving all footpaths in a hopelessly overgrown and neglected state.

ROUTE 33. THE ASCENT OF CERRO DEL CABALLO FROM LANJARÓN

Figures: 28km/2300m (including descent)

Cerro del Caballo (Hill of the Horse) was once a very popular objective with visitors to the spa town of Lanjarón, especially on horseback. The route up the Valle del Lanjarón afforded easy passage to four-legged transport and an excellent cobbled path (Camino de la Sierra) was built, penetrating deep into the valley before climbing in zig-zags via the Tello forest house to the Ventura hut. This path has now fallen into, if not disuse then certainly infrequent use. However, it is still usable and its cobbled surface has survived remarkably well as far as the bridge over the river below Casa Forestal del Tello.

The number of farms on the slopes of this valley means that there are paths all over the valley sides, and the Camino de la Sierra encounters many junctions. Generally the Camino keeps left, but the giveaway clue is the cobbles. If they disappear for more than a couple of hundred metres you have taken a wrong turning.

At the eastern end of Lanjarón's main street is the bridge over the Rio Lanjarón. The path commences on the eastern bank of the river as a broad track. Within 100m, take a turning on the right which climbs steeply in zig-zags with the distinctive cobbled surface to a junction. The main path seems to bend around to the right along with its cobbles, but the Camino de la Sierra is the left branch continuing straight ahead. The cobbles soon reappear under a patina of moss and lichen. The Camino is now easy to follow for a while, winding its way up among luxuriant vegetation.

Shortly, the path enters an area of 'cortijos' and is almost lost among a multitude of farm tracks. The Camino de la Sierra continues purposefully up-valley and the cobbles are once again the best way to identify its course.

Once clear of the farms the path becomes more distinct and continuous and soon emerges into an open, treeless area. At the far side of this area the broad track sweeps around uphill to the right, but the way to Caballo lies along a smaller path branching left to pass by the back of a ramshackle farm building (makeshift signpost to 'Tello').

The path now descends in a loop among delectable surroundings, crosses a picturesque little footbridge over the river with a waterfall above, and then commences a steep zig-zag ascent through pine woods to the Casa Forestal del Tello.

Casa Tello occupies a secluded spot, embowered in trees with pleasant grassy swards all around. At the edge of the forest, overlooking the river, a good (but depressingly distant) view of Caballo can be obtained. The onward route lies behind the building to the north.

Ignore a plain path in front of the building heading south-west as this leads only to the network of jeep tracks on Caballo's south ridge.

The next section is navigationally the most difficult part of the ascent. The crux is to reach the ruins of the Ventura hut, at the edge of the trees and at the beginning of the long final drag up the flank of the ridge to the summit. The problem is that the zig-zags of the path in the forest are rather indistinct and are often thickly carpeted with pine needles. By following a line slightly to the west of north, you will cross a farm track and a path will eventually be picked up which will lead to the hut ruins.

From here the route is straightforward. A good path ascends the flank of the main ridge and leads via the utterly ruined Lanjarón hut to the tiny Refugio del Caballo. The way to the top from the refuge lies around the south side of the brooding Laguna del Caballo to ascend a steep scree path to a col on the north side of the summit dome, from where it is an easy matter to walk up the easy slope to the highest point.

The 3009m summit - the most westerly 3000-er in the Sierra Nevada - is perhaps not the mountain top you deserve after such a long climb, being a simple dome with a trig pillar and a thick carpet of goat droppings, but it is undoubtedly a superb viewpoint. The panorama is extensive but is not seen at its best in summer when heat haze severely restricts visibility.

A short cut is possible in descent by heading due south through the Hoya del Zorro ('zorro' = a fox) to the ruins of the Refugio de Lanjarón, thence rejoining the path to the Ventura hut.

ROUTE 34. THE ASCENT OF MULHACÉN FROM TREVÉLEZ

Figures: 17km/2000m (including descent)

Now out of favour as a summer ascent route due to much easier access to the summit via the Sierra Nevada roads, this old classic route - once the 'ruta normal' up the mountain - still makes an excellent climb, especially in winter.

It seems logical that Trevélez, being the highest village in the country, should be the most convenient base for the ascent of Mulhacén, the highest mountain, and the altitude of the village leaves only 2000m of mountain to be climbed. This cuts the mountain down to a manageable size, but feels less of a cheat than does driving up to the foot of the west flank on the South Road, or even worse, to the summit car park.

From the higher 'barrio' of Trevélez, a small path ascends the shallow valley of the Rio Chico de Trevélez heading for the bulky hump of El Chorillo, which dominates the skyline. After a short, but fairly steep, climb the valley is crossed by an old 'acequia' (irrigation channel), just below 1900m. Leave the valley bed here and ascend leftwards (west) below the craggy slopes of Tajos del Chorillo.

A long and stony climb now leads to the broad back of the Loma del Tanto close to the 2722m summit of El Chorillo. The dirt road and a popular parking area are here encountered, and it is likely to be a busy place in the summer months. In winter, it will be deserted.

The massive bulk of Mulhacén lies to the north, with the long ridge of the Loma del Tanto/Loma del Mulhacén leading up at an easy angle to the distant summit. Do not underestimate the amount of work still to be done. From this point to the summit is over 5km even by the most direct line, and there is still almost 800m of height to be gained, all of it at potentially breathless altitude.

Even if the road is not snow-covered, it is not worth using it on foot because its route meanders considerably in search of the easiest gradients, covering an extra 2¹/₂km compared with a direct line. The ridge is rough and rocky in places, but is very broad, and nowhere difficult. It allows relatively easy progress and a steady uphill plod will eventually bring the summit underfoot.

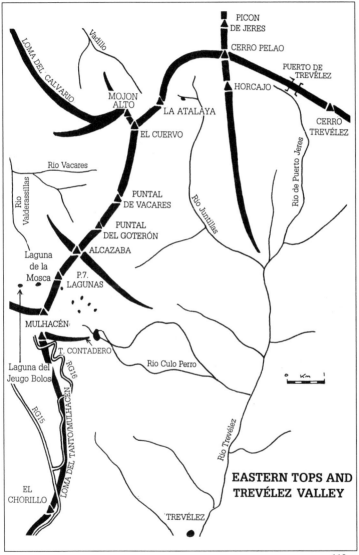

EASTERN TOPS AND TREVÉLEZ VALLEY

Arrival at the top is dramatic. After the expansive slopes of the south side it is a shock to suddenly come upon the edge of the precipices of the northern escarpment. The ridge ends abruptly at the very edge of the 700m Pared Norte (North Wall), with spectacular views down into the Genil valley and along the main ridge, westwards to Veleta and north-east to the ragged bulk of Alcazaba.

A descent via the Cañada de las Siete Lagunas, Rio Culo del Perro and Rio Trevélez is possible, but this would make a very long and arduous outing. Another possible variation is a descent of the west flank to the South Sierra Nevada Road and then an easy walk along the road back to El Chorillo, but this has little to recommend it over a return along the ridge.

ROUTE 35. TO CAÑADA DE LAS SIETE LAGUNAS VIA RIO CULO DEL PERRO FROM TREVÉLEZ

Figures: 18km/1450m (to Laguna Hondera and back)

The Cañada de las Siete Lagunas is a superb place for wild camping and makes a good base camp for ascents of Mulhacén and Alcazaba as well as the more remote peaks to the north-east. It can be reached from Trevélez via a good path across the western slopes of the Trevélez valley into valley of the oddly named Rio Culo de Perro (Dog's Arse River) and then climbing the latter valley to its head in the Cañada. The route is straightforward, but it is worth remembering that the floor of the Cañada lies between 2900 and 3100m thus making the climb equivalent to the ascent of one of the range's major peaks. A good impression of the size of Mulhacén and Alcazaba is gained when you have toiled from 1500m to 3000m only to have them still towering over you on either side.

From Trevélez Barrio Alto, follow a good path which climbs diagonally across the western slopes of the main valley, passing through a much cultivated area known as Prados Grandes to eventually curve around into the obvious side-valley of the Rio Culo de Perro. The path climbs into the valley and then follows the stream as it ascends through a little wooded ravine. At 2500m above sea level, the valley climbs clear of the trees and enters an easier angled section heading for the daunting-looking cascades of Chorreras Negras, which are the last obstacle before reaching the bed of the Cañada at the Laguna Hondera. The cascades are picturesque and although steep, the escarpment gives no difficulty to the scrambler.

At the top of the waterfalls the Cañada de las Siete Lagunas is suddenly revealed, rising steadily towards a final steep slope to the main ridge with the tiny peak of Puntal de Siete Lagunas perched atop the headwall and dwarfed between the massive architecture of Mulhacén and Alcazaba on either hand like a small child between obese parents. Note that on the IGN map the Puntal de Siete Lagunas is wrongly labelled. The peak given the name (3322m) is actually one of Alcazaba's subsidiary tops, while the unnamed little peak to the south-west (3255m) is the real P.7 Lagunas.

The first of the lagunas to be encountered is the shallow pool of Laguna Hondera at 2900m. This, the lowest laguna, is only one of two of the seven to be named. The other, Laguna Altera, is the highest of the seven and is tucked up close below Puntal de Siete Lagunas at 3060m. In between lie the other five, scattered across the floor of the cañada, connected by rushing streams and surrounded by grassy swards. Just pick your pitch.

ROUTE 36. ASCENT OF ALCAZABA FROM CAÑADA DE LAS SIETE LAGUNAS

Figures: 7km/500m (from Laguna Hondera to summit and back)

Alcazaba, like Mulhacén, offers easier approaches away from the main ridge. The best starting point is Laguna Hondera, from where you can follow a fairly indistinct but easy ridge which rises without difficulty to the top of the forbidding band of crags overlooking the upper Cañada de las Siete Lagunas.

From the Laguna, head initially NNE across a flat area to the foot of the ridge. As the ground begins to rise, veer north-west to climb directly up the easy but rough spur. Rocks and boulders (some loose) lead up above the crags, passing a subsidiary top at 3288m and bringing you to a flattish area below the summit ridge, which runs north-easterly. The summit pyramid is clearly visible and a superb traverse of the rocky ridge, with superb views to the west ridge, leads to the peak at 3371m.

ROUTE 37. ASCENT OF MULHACÉN FROM CAÑADA DE LAS SIETE LAGUNAS

Figures: 4km/580m (from Laguna Hondera to summit and back)

Mulhacén presents a formidable face to the 7 Lagunas valley. A massive wall of broken crags and scree, there is no easy way up it. The obvious line is a huge scree chute which descends from the summit to a point about halfway between Laguna Hondera and Laguna Altera, in the midst of the lesser Lagunas. This chute leads unerringly to the summit and a detailed description is superfluous. However, I should mention that the ascent of this scree during summer is extremely trying, as it is the most treacherous sliding variety you could wish to encounter. The slope is composed of stones which vary from gravelly to the size of a washing machine, and all have an equal propensity for sliding slowly towards the floor of the Cañada.

Undoubtedly, the best time to make this climb is early or late in the season, when snow may give easier passage. In winter, crampons and ice axe are obviously essential.

ROUTE 38. TREVÉLEZ TO JERES DEL MARQUESADO VIA PUERTO DE TREVÉLEZ

Figures: 25km/1325m (one way trip)
MBF

The Puerto de Trevélez is one of the Sierra Nevada's most ancient and important foot passes. In times past it was an important trade route linking the Alpujarras with Guadix, and it is still much used by walkers even today.

As routes in these mountains go it is an easy walk, but don't underestimate the distance to be covered, and remember that the col itself is almost 2800m above sea level, entailing a long climb and descent. In summer, and especially if carrying a heavy pack, an early start is a must.

Mountain bikers will obviously make faster progress, especially on the descent to Jeres, but the final ascent to the pass is rather steep, and most will opt for an easy push rather than a gruelling ride.

The route commences up the Trevélez valley along the good path named the Camino de Granada. Keep left at junctions, avoiding the tempting paths climbing across the eastern side of the valley, as these gradually become indistinct as they gain height. The main path soon reaches the valley bed, crosses the river and continues along the east bank.

About 4km from Trevélez the valley narrows and begins to climb more steeply, soon passing the mouth of the Rio Culo de Perro on the left.

Rising relentlessly, the valley becomes more featureless as it continues as a straight and narrow trench, enclosed by steep slopes.

At the junction with the Rio Juntillas, the path begins its determined climb towards the Puerto, forsaking the river which now splits into various 'barrancos' and striking across the slopes above one of the streams.

After a testing 800m ascent, the path reaches the barren col at 2798m where a superb view of the Marquesado forest comes into view. To the north-west, the broad and easy main ridge leads up to Cerro Pelao (Bald Hill) - the first of the 3000-ers - while to the south-east the simplest of walks leads to the summit of Cerro de Trevélez (2878m) at the beginning of a long ridge stretching east over a number of sub-3000m hills to Puerto de la Ragua. These eastern lower summits make an excellent winter outing on nordic ski, being smooth, easy angled and broad topped, and having superb views all around.

The descent from the Puerto de Trevélez to Jeres is long but very easy, and seems made for mountain bikes in summer, and skis in winter. Walkers will find it rather long, especially under a summer sun, but the views on the upper half are tremendous, and the shade of the trees lower down makes the final stages a little easier.

The good path heads directly down the Loma de Enmedio,

descending 1200m over a distance of 8km - not especially steep, but relentless. Just above 1500m the path reaches the Marquesado del Zenete forest track (RG19). Turning left along this track will take you around the Barranco Alhori to the Casa Forestal del Porterillo. At this point, the path from Jeres crosses the track en route to Picon de Jeres. This path leads easily down to Jeres through rich, cultivated country, the surroundings becoming more lush and green with every metre of descent.

Jeres itself is rather disappointing. The grand title leads you to expect a picturesque little village, but in truth the place is merely a haphazard group of scattered buildings.

ROUTE 39. ASCENT OF CERRO PELAO FROM JERES DEL MARQUESADO

Figures: 15km/1970m (with descent via Puerto de Trevélez)

The ascent of Cerro Pelao is not often undertaken for its own sake, for it is a long and fairly arduous climb and the summit is dull and featureless. It is more often the first objective on the traverse of the whole of the main ridge - the Integral de los Tres Mil (Route 45) - when it is the obvious way onto the end of the ridge from Jeres.

However, combined with Picon de Jeres and Horcajo de Trevélez it provides a pleasant way to bag a trio of 3000-ers, with none of the trying rocks and scree found further along the watershed. Descent can be made via Puerto de Trevélez to provide a round trip if desired.

Leave Jeres by the road heading for Lanteira. The road heads south-west at first, but loops around to the east, crossing the Arroyo de Jeres. Just before the bridge over the Arroyo, a dirt track heads off up the valley, leading to the Casa Forestal del Porterillo. Follow this track to the Casa, situated on the Marquesado del Zenete dirt track (RG19), which contours across the slopes of the eastern lower Sierra Nevada at about 1500m.

From Porterillo, head slightly south of west (no path initially) for 100m to reach a broad firebreak which leads all the way to the upper limit of the forest at c.2500m. Above the treeline, slopes of extremely prickly 'pin cushion plants' lead up towards the ridge. These slopes are often roamed by bullocks which bear an uncomfortable resemblance to young fighting bulls, but they seem far too contented to bother with any kind of strenuous activity. Even red shorts and rucksacks go unnoticed.

The skyline descends northwards from Picon de Jeres to a prominent hump on the ridge - Mirador Alto (High Viewpoint). Aim to reach the ridge between this hump and the top of Picon, thence following the broad ridge-crest to the summit.

The summit of Picon de Jeres (3090m) is really just a small flat area on the generally rising ridge to Cerro Pelao (3141m), which is easily reached by a simple uphill walk along the stony crest.

The main ridge now stretches away to the south-west over the shattered rock crests of Cervatillos, Atalaya and El Cuervo, with Alcazaba and Veleta jutting skywards in the distance, but branching south is a short side spur carrying the summit of Horcajo de Trevélez (3179m). Labelling on local maps is woefully inaccurate in this area, especially on the IGN map where Horcajo is given the name Cerro Pelado, while Cerro Pelao is unnamed. I have adhered to the names accepted locally.

An alternative to retracing your upward steps to Jeres is provided by the route via Puerto de Trevélez and the Loma de Enmedio (see Route 38). There are two variations on the descent to the Puerto. From Cerro Pelao, the ridge over the subsidiary summit of Piedra de los Ladrones is the obvious way, but if on the summit of Horcajo de Trevélez, a shorter alternative is provided by a broad spur dropping due east from the top. Descend this spur for 250m then make a descending traverse around the head of the Hoya del Toro ('toro' = bull!) to reach the col.

PART 4

Longer and Multi-day Routes

INTRODUCTION

You would expect a mountain range such as this, with between 20 and 30 summits over 3000m (depending on whose definition you subscribe to), to have possibilities for longer days out and also multi-day backpacking trips. The Sierra Nevada will not disappoint. The six routes described below are merely a suggested selection from the almost limitless possibilities. One of them is a well established classic, but the others are my own inventions, though the 'Big Three' must be an obvious challenge to any determined peak bagger.

The long-day routes assume a high level of fitness, competence, and motivation, as well as good conditions. Winter elevates all these routes - with the exception of Route 42 - to expedition status. Conversely, Route 42 will be very arduous in summer when temperatures at low altitudes can top 40°C. The multi-day routes are split into fairly relaxed day stages (mentioned in the route description) and there is no reason why the day routes could not be tackled in more leisurely fashion over two days; see the descriptions for suggested camp/bivouac sites.

ROUTE 40. THE EASTERN 3000-ers FROM TREVÉLEZ

Figures: 40km/2100m (including all summits)

The eastern end of the 3000m sector has a different character to the western or central sections. The western end is developed and popular - largely because of the ski-resort - and the central section (Mulhacén to Vacares) is on a much grander scale, and much more rugged. The eastern 3000-ers, in contrast, are quite and unspoilt.

The formidable barrier of Mulhacén and Alcazaba keeps them safe from the day-trippers in the west, while the lack of convenient vehicular approaches ensures that only serious hillgoers will be met on these summits. It is odd to think that Mulhacén - the highest mountain in Spain - is visited by dozens of summer trippers each day, some of them driving their cars to within a few metres of the top, while the comparatively insignificant summit of El Cuervo is trodden only by the feet of a few dedicated hillwalkers, and only after a suitable amount of collar work has been done to earn it.

From Trevélez, follow Route 38 to attain the Puerto de Trevélez, at the eastern end of the 3000m sector. Turn left and ascend the easy ridge over the summit of Piedra de los Ladrones to Cerro Pelao (3141m). The ridge hereabouts is flat-topped and stony, with spurs leading off to Picón de Jeres (3090m) northwards and to Horcajo de Trevélez (3179m) southwards. Both are easily reached in a few minutes' walking.

The main ridge now heads off to the west, easily at first, but becoming rougher as it traverses the multiple summits of Cervatillos (highest top 3112m). Veering south-west, the ridge, now a jumble of boulders, climbs gradually to the top of La Buitrera (3151m) which is wrongly labelled as Pico del Cuervo on the IGN map. The ridge has now become very rough, and much time is spent clambering over huge splintered masses of rock - don't be fooled by the smooth contours shown on local maps, nothing could be further from the truth.

A descent into a shallow col followed by a gentle 40m ascent brings you to the summit of La Atalaya (The Watchtower) at 3143m, a peak which fails to live up to the promise held in its imposing title. The summit is a bouldery ridge quite unlike the battlemented viewing platform suggested by the name.

Now the ridge dips below 3000m for the first time since Cerro Pelao. A bouldery descent leads to the narrow Collado del Cuervo at the foot of a steep and rocky 150m climb to the 3148m summit of El Cuervo (The Raven) with its elegant tall cairn. Ignore the names given to cols and peaks on the IGN map which is completely confused; the cartographer must have drawn this section after a particularly bibulous siesta.

El Cuervo has a satelite summit - Mojón Alto - which lies to the north-west at the end of a short, easy ridge. Its 3118m summit is worth visiting for the superb view down the long Calvarios ridge into the profound vee of the Genil valley.

Descending from El Cuervo to the next col (Cuneta de Vacares) is rather awkward. The ridge narrows to a jagged crest with a couple of steep steps, making it necessary to descend unpleasant scree slopes on the western side. These slopes will lead you down into a little canyon to the north-west of the Cuneta, with a rare patch of grass and evidence of overnight camping. This is, in fact, a popular first bivouac site for parties attempting the Integral de los Tres Mil (Route 45).

From Cuneta de Vacares, the ridge climbs to the escarpment which leads to Alcazaba. Puntal de Vacares, the first top on this escarpment, is worth a visit for its impressive view of Alcazaba, but if planning to return to Trevélez today, then it would be best to descend from the Cuneta.

Directly below the col lies the Laguna de Vacares, which has a legend about an enchantress who is reputed to live below its dark waters, and who will cast a spell on anyone who sleeps on its shores. A nice story, but one whose validity I have not managed to investigate.

From the Laguna, follow the shallow valley of its issuing stream (almost always dry) which leads to a long but uneventful descent of the Rio Juntillas. The Juntillas joins the Rio Trevélez at the foot of the south ridge of Horcajo de Trevélez, and steps can then be retraced along the good path in the valley to the village, some 8km downstream.

ROUTE 41. ESTACION DE SAN JUAN TO TREVÉLEZ VIA CUNETA DE VACARES

Figures: 26km/1780m (one way trip)

This route is one of a number of possible crossings from the Genil to the Alpujarras. However, it is the easiest, and probably the quickest alternative. Others, which go via Valdecasillas/Cañada de las Siete Lagunas, or via Valdecasillas/South Sierra Nevada Road,

Climbing the Veredon Superior *(Photo by Ian Roberts)*
The Elorrieta hut

Above:
Sierra Nevada Road at 3100m. Veleta and the start of the Veredon Superior path in the middle of the picture

Right:
The summit of El Cuervo looking to Alcazaba and Mulhacén

have rougher terrain and, in the case of the latter, the often overcrowded road to contend with.

This route, via Cuesta del Calvarios, Prados de Vacares, the Cuneta, Rio Juntillas, and Rio Trevélez needs no detailed description as the ascent to the pass is covered in Routes 15 and 16, and the descent to Trevélez is described above (Route 40). The way is generally obvious and although long, there is no reason why it could not be accomplished in a day, even if heavily laden.

ROUTE 42. A TOUR OF BAJA MONTAÑA. FROM CORTIJO SEVILLA

Figures: 44km/2800m (incl. Los Alayos and climbing Trevenque last)

A number of alternative tours of Baja Montaña are possible, some including the Alayos de Dilar, some excluding them. I have chosen this one because it covers all the main peaks of the area but allows shorter escape routes if you find you've bitten off more than you can chew. The inclusion of Los Alayos would almost certainly make the route too long for a day walk for most people, though that may be like a red rag to those who are overflowing with animal strength and determination.

Starting from Cortijo Sevilla on the Huenes valley forestry road (RG9), follow Route 3 via Fuente Fria to the summit of Cerro Huenes. Head now across the scrubby plateau to the gravelly cone of Cerro Gordo (part of Route 4 in reverse). From the peaked top of Gordo, descend eastwards onto a ridge which will lead you over two small summits to reach a broad track at the pronounced col of El Collado at the foot of Cerro del Cocón, which is easily reached by a short steep climb up its gravelly southern slope.

Route 8 can now be used to traverse Cerro de la Cortijuela to the Collado de Ruquino and ascend Pico del Tesoro. The head of the Huenes valley is dominated by the huge bulk of the Loma de Dilar, descending from Veleta, and it is better to descend from Tesoro to the forestry road at Casa de la Cortijuela via the Collado de Matas Verdes. The 'fuente' at Cortijuela is a source of superb drinking water and should be taken advantage of - water of this quality is not plentiful on the remainder of the route.

From Cortijuela, follow the dirt road as it meanders up through the pines to the Collado del Trevenque then descends to the two small buildings at Collado de Chaquetas. The road gives easy walking, and few vehicles will be met on this farthest drivable stretch. Most motorists go no further than the botanical garden at Cortijuela. NOTE: As you approach Collado del Trevenque the peak of Trevenque itself is close at hand and could be visited in a steep but short 45min detour (Route 6), saving yourself the long climb to the summit from the Dilar at the end of the walk.

From Chaquetas, Route 12 will take you onto the Los Alayos ridge, but if including this complex ridge an overnight stop will likely be required. The best place for such a stop would be by the Rio Dilar below the Collado de Chaquetas. The area near the footbridge is sheltered, has patches of good grass and its position neatly splits the route into two fairly moderate days of effort.

Follow Route 12 to the summit ridge of El Castillejos and continue along the ridge to the final peak of Picacho Alto, overlooking the clearing at Los Miradores (see Routes 10 and 13). The return leg can be simplified by following the traversing path along the north flanks of the ridge, descending finally via the Cuesta del Pino to the Dilar valley near La Toma. If you elected to bag Trevenque via the short steep eastern slope earlier on the route, then all that remains is an easy walk along the gentle path via Barranco del Búho to return to Cortijo Sevilla. If, however, you chose to save the 'king peak' until last you may now be regretting the decision; there is serious toil still to be undertaken.

Consult the description of Route 7 for information on the climb from the Dilar bed to the sandy valley of Las Arenales, but instead of following the 1992 dirt road extension all the way to the Chaquetas goat station, turn off onto the Las Arenales path where it branches from the track just before crossing the Barranco de Aguas Blanquillas (Ravine of Little White Waters), which is actually almost always dry.

Upon reaching the sands of Las Arenales head east, passing the curious finger called La Esfinge and aiming for the obvious green slope directly below the summit. The ascent of the soft sand to reach the old jeep track at the foot of Trevenque's final pyramid is hard work, especially in summer when reflected heat from the sand puts you in mind of old film scenes of legionnaires staggering across Saharan dunes gasping for water. Make sure you are carrying plenty!

When the foot of the final upthrust is reached, follow Route 5 to the top, from where you can survey the panorama of all the peaks you have just traversed. This view alone makes it worthwhile leaving Trevenque until last. Descent to Cortijo Sevilla via the Cuerda del Trevenque (Route 5) is all that remains to be done, and an easy walk down this descending ridge makes a fitting end to this tour of the Sierra Nevada's 'low mountains'.

ROUTE 43. EL TRIO GRANDE (THE BIG THREE) FROM ESTACION DE SAN JUAN

Figures: 42km/3200m

The trio grande of the Sierra Nevada are Mulhacén (3483m), Veleta (3394m), and Alcazaba (3371m). Although there are more than twenty summits over 3000m in the range, these three stand head and shoulders above the rest, not just in height but in character too. They have the biggest crags, the most imposing forms and the greatest presence. Among the high Sierra they are pre-eminent.

The bagging of El Trio Grande in one expedition is a natural challenge, but even fit individuals will need two days to accomplish it. As you would expect from peaks of this stature, none of the three is attained easily. Scree and crags provide formidable obstacles and considerable fortitude will no doubt be called upon. An overnight stay at the Felix Mendez hut or a camp nearby is the most logical halfway halt, but even to reach here from San Juan in one day is an arduous undertaking. The alternative would be a wild camp in the Cañada de las Siete Lagunas, but this would leave a longer second day. You takes your choice...

From Estacion de San Juan, Alcazaba is your first objective, but the peak is a thorny problem as befits its character. There are two alternative ascent routes. Either a) use Routes 15/17 to reach the ridge at the Collado de Siete Lagunas then consult Route 31 for the way to the top, or b) follow Routes 15/16 to reach Tajos del Goteron, then circumvent the end of the crag to ascend to the summit.

Alternative b) will appeal to the purist because it allows a north-east to south-west traverse of the peak, but alternative a) is a great deal more straightforward, has better scenery, and is shorter to boot.

Assuming you have used alternative a) and reached the summit, retrace your steps into the Cañada de las Siete Lagunas and gird up your loins for the ascent of the 500m of scree which lie between the Cañada and the summit of Spain (see Route 37). From the top of Mulhacén, an easy descent of the western flank and a stroll along the South Sierra Nevada Road will take you to the Refugio de Felix Mendez.

From a perusal of the map, the obvious way to Veleta lies over the top of Los Machos and the connecting ridge, but this is a blind alley. The ridge becomes very difficult, and the final step below Veleta's summit is a vertical crag, totally impassable to all but rock-climbers. The only way to the top for walkers is to follow the South Sierra Nevada Road to the Veleta col. Using the dirt track does detract from the character of the route but the ridge and its flanking slope is just too inhospitable to be worthwhile. The final double hairpin can be short-cutted but resist the temptation to traverse above the road below Veleta's crags unless you enjoy struggling over loose boulders while being bombarded from above by cola cans from the car trippers on the summit.

At the col, leave the road and climb easily up the south-west ridge to join the cars and trippers on the top of the Sierra Nevada's second highest mountain.

Now all that remains is the walk down to San Juan. The map suggests that a direct descent of the Loma de San Juan is the obvious way, but this is not recommended. The lower slopes of the ridge are cluttered with private farms which have 'prohibido el paso' (prohibited passage) signs and numerous barking dogs - a fairly effective deterrent. It is possible to follow the ridge as far as the headland of Atalayon Grande (see Route 22) and then make a rough descent due east into the Guarnón valley, but even this has little to recommend it.

The best way down is to descend the north ridge (the upper part of the Loma de San Juan) until you meet the Sierra Nevada Road at about 3100m then use the Verdon Superior to gain access to the bed of the Corral del Veleta (see Route 23). From the Corral a straightforward descent of the Guarnón valley (Route 20 in reverse) will take you to the Vereda de la Estrella which leads pleasantly back to San Juan.

ROUTE 44. A TOUR OF SIERRA NEVADA FROM TREVÉLEZ

Figures: 56km/5400m

Backpackers will be able to plan their own 'tours' of the Sierra Nevada by looking at the map, and linking together sections of the routes described in this guide. The scope for variation is huge. The tour described below is merely a suggestion.

From Trevélez, ascend the valley of the Rio Trevélez to the junction with the Rio Juntillas then ascend the valley of the Juntillas almost to the forest limit. Just below the last few trees, turn up a small dry tributary on the left heading slightly north of west. This will lead you up a long and tedious climb to the Laguna de Vacares, just below the main ridge (see Routes 38, 39, 40 and 41 for further information on this section of the walk).

Climb westward from the laguna to cross the ridge at the Cuneta de Vacares, then head north-west across the flank of the Calvarios ridge. After approx 2km paths will be met (various levels) which gradually converge on the grassy shelf on which the Calvarios forestry hut and the ruins of the Choza del Tio Papeles stand. From here, a network of good paths descends the wooded slope on the Genil side of the ridge (Cuesta del Calvarios or Presidarios) to the stone and concrete footbridge (Puente del Burro) by the Vadillo bivouac hut. This is a good spot to spend the night (though I find a tent preferable to the hut) having covered approximately 21km and 1500m of ascent since leaving Trevélez.

Next morning, climb up the steep path from the hut to join the Vereda de la Estrella and turn left to follow it to the ruins of the

Cortijo de la Estrella at the foot of the Guarnón barranco. Route 20 will now guide you up to the Corral del Veleta, from where the Veredon Superior can be climbed to reach Veleta's north ridge (see Route 23 for a description of the Veredon Superior). Now scramble exhilaratingly up the soaring ridge to the peaked top of Veleta.

It is a pity that the direct traverse of the main ridge to Los Machos is too difficult for walkers. It would make a superb way to reach the Collado de Valdeinfiernos but the big crag below Veleta's summit would demand an abseil descent, which is outside the scope of this book. The only alternative for walkers is to descend the south-west ridge to the Collado de la Carijuela, where the Sierra Nevada Road crosses the watershed, and then follow the road to the Collado de Valdeinfiernos, just beyond Los Machos. Perhaps a case could be made for a Dolomites style Via Ferrata iron ladder to be installed on Veleta; after all, they have already built a road up the other side!

From the Collado, a tiny path wriggles down the scree into the Valdeinfiernos corral and it is then a simple matter to follow the valley down to the Cueva Secreta, a good overnight halt. The second day of this tour has involved about 19km and a total of 2050m of uphill.

Day three commences with the ascent of the Loma de las Casillas (Route 18) which leads unerringly to the summit of Juego Bolos (3022m) and then links up with the main ridge at the superb peak of Puntal de la Caldera (3225m). From the summit of Caldera, dwarfed under Mulhacén's west flank, follow the ridge eastward to the Collado del Mulhacén from where there is a superb view into the Hoya del Mulhacén with the huge Pared Norte (North Wall) looming on the right. The west ridge/flank now gives an easy climb to the summit of the great peak with dizzying views through gaps overlooking the Hoya. The Pared Norte is not a continuous crag. It consists of a series of rock bands and buttresses, linked together by a system of scree ledges and gullies. In winter these ledges and gullies form excellent snow climbs which are not technically difficult, but very exposed. The total height of the face is 700m.

From the summit of Mulhacén, a simple walk down the south ridge to El Chorillo and a descent eastwards into the valley of the Rio Chico de Trevélez (Route 34) will return you to your starting point. Day three's figures are 16km and 1850m of climb.

ROUTE 45. THE INTEGRAL DE LOS TRES MIL. FROM JERES DEL MARQUESADO TO LANJARÓN

Figures: 58km/1400m Three or four days

The Integral is the classic Sierra Nevada peak-bagging expedition, and is often undertaken by youth groups and Spanish military parties. These expeditions usually take three days, sometimes four, and include overnight stops at Cuneta de Vacares, Cañada de las Siete Lagunas, Refugio de Felix Mendez, or occasionally at Las Yeguas.

Strictly speaking, Integral de los Tres Mil means 'the whole of the three thousands' and thus should include a visit to every 3000m summit of the range. However, Spanish parties often refer to the route as the Ruta Alta (High Route) and it is then considered acceptable to bypass the worst sections of ridge, such as Puntal de la Caldera and Tajos de la Virgen, and omit outlying summits, such as Horcajo de Trevélez, Mojón Alto and Juego Bolos.

The route I describe here is a purist Integral, but the Ruta Alta short cuts are referred to as and when they are encountered.

Be sure to carry plenty of liquid with you as sources of fresh water are not plentiful on the ridge, and detours to obtain it will make an already arduous trip even more difficult. This is especially true in winter, when there will be little or no meltwater available.

From Jeres, use Route 39 to reach the bald summit of Cerro Pelao via Picón de Jeres. A short detour to collect Horcajo should be made before heading west over the bouldery summits of Cervatillos and La Buitrera (The Vulture's Nest). The ridge curves south to the undistinguished summit of La Atalaya, before making a sharp descent on blocks of mica schist to Collado del Cuervo (Col of the Raven), and a steep 150m climb to the summit of El Cuervo.

Another detour is now required to visit the summit of Mojón Alto to the north-west and you can then head for Cuneta de Vacares and the first possible bivouac site. The descent from Cuervo to the Cuneta is made awkward by big steps on the ridge crest and it is necessary to use scree slopes on the west side to avoid the difficulty (see Route 40 for a fuller description of the traverse of these eastern

Puntal de Vacares and the first bivouac site on the Ruta Alta

tops).

If you have time in hand, you may prefer to continue over Alcazaba and make your first camp in the Cañada de las Siete Lagunas, but Alcazaba is time-consuming. Allow a minimum of 2 hours to go from Cuneta to Cañada.

Beyond the Cuneta, the ridge rises sharply to the summit of Puntal de Vacares and continues rockily to the pinnacled top of Puntal del Goterón which is almost in the shadow of Alcazaba's huge bulk. The direct line of the ridge to Alcazaba is barred by an overhanging band of crag - Tajos del Goterón. This crag forms a continuous barrier which runs diagonally across almost the whole of the north-east face of the mountain. There are only two possible ways of circumventing this obstacle. The first is to follow the linking ridge until almost at the foot of the crag, then traverse rightwards along the Gran Vasar (Great Shelf), which runs across the north face at about 3000m. A short way along this shelf, a series of steep gullies leads up to rejoin the ridge above the big step. However, these gullies are unpleasant in summer (loose scree) and in winter they carry a 'Dificil' (difficult) grading. The second alternative, more suitable for walkers but much more time-consuming, is to make a descending traverse leftwards to round the toe of the crag at its south-eastern extremity (c.2900m) and then climb laboriously up almost 500m of scree.

Once on the summit, the even greater mass of Mulhacén looms into view. Luckily, the crags on Mulhacén's east face are not so continuous as Alcazaba's, and ways through them can be found relatively easily. If you are intending to spend a night in the Cañada de las Siete Lagunas, then the obvious line onto Mulhacén is the more southerly scree chute described in Route 37, but if continuing directly between Alcazaba and Mulhacén then a line closer to the main ridge can be utilised. Don't forget to visit the little peak of Puntal de Siete Lagunas, on the ridge between the two.

Alcazaba presents difficulties on its south-west face, too, and it is necessary to make a slight detour away from the main ridge to the east, where a broad scree chute will be found which can be descended until below the crags. Now traverse back westwards to rejoin the main ridge near Puntal de Siete Lagunas.

Mulhacén's north-east ridge has a big step - well described by

The summit pinnacle of Puntal del Goterón

Collomb as a 'cockscomb' - but this is easily avoided by scree gullies on the left, which give access to the upper ridge, a jagged mass of jumbled boulders. Clambering over these huge blocks, superb views down the north face can be obtained. Although many of the routes on the Pared Norte are not technically difficult, the exposure is considerable, something which will be well appreciated from this viewpoint.

The summit is reached without difficulty and don't be surprised if it is occupied; during summer, it is not unusual to find enduro motorbikes, or people in shirt-sleeves and shiny town shoes on the top. Thanks to the building of the dirt road to the summit ridge, this highest piece of ground in Spain suffers all manner of indignities at the hands of the day tripper. It goes without saying that litter on the summit is on the increase.

An easy descent of the west ridge brings you to the Mulhacén col. The High Route descends the west flank and then follows the road to the Felix Mendez hut, but if sticking to the Integral route it is necessary to visit the summits of Juego Bolos, Puntal de la Caldera and Loma Pela. The first of these is reached by descending a steep slope on the right, just before reaching the top of Caldera, which gives access to the connecting ridge, then retracing your steps to the main ridge to 'collect' Caldera.

The summit ridge of Caldera has a big notch, which is circumvented by descending rocky steps on the north side, passing through the notch to the south side, and then scrambling across awkward slabs to pick up a path which climbs up to the shallow saddle between Loma Pela's two summits. The southern summit is only one metre higher (3188m) than the northern top, but the latter is by far the better viewpoint.

The next section of the main ridge is the Crestones de Rio Seco, and its sharp, jagged pinnacles are totally impractical to traverse - even the dedicated Integral-er will choose to bypass this section. Luckily, the road runs close to the crest at this point, and it is easy to descend from Loma Pela to the road and follow it to the Felix Mendez hut, which makes a convenient second night stopping place. Camping is permitted in the Rio Seco corral in the area surrounding the hut, but only with the hut warden's permission.

Day three commences with more walking along the road. The

The formidable barrier of Tajos del Goterón on the north-east side of Alcazaba

sharks-teeth profile of the Crestones continues all the way to the foot of Los Machos, but the highest of the 'teeth' can be visited by a short scramble. After rejoining the road from Felix Mendez, follow it as it passes through a man-made notch in the Raspones de Rio Seco ridge, which branches off southwards at this point, and the next pinnacle ahead on the crest is the highest (3156m on IGN map) of the Crestones. Its splintered top gives a dizzying view into the Corral de Valdeinfiernos.

The mass of Los Machos now towers ahead, and you must now leave the road to climb to its summit up the scree-covered east buttress (Route 28). Los Machos, fourth highest summit of the Sierra Nevada, is a good viewpoint, but lacks any distinctive 'personality' of its own. It is really only the end of Veleta's eastern shoulder, but its broad slabby top is a complete contrast to Veleta's jutting prow, and it can boast some magnificent crags overlooking Valdeinfiernos which have climbing routes up to 'Dificil' grade, with some winter ice pitches as high as Grade 5.

The purist Integral-er now has a dilemma to grapple with. The ridge to Veleta has three named summits: Campanario, Zacatin and

Salon. They are really pinnacles, and some quite exposed scrambling on insecure rock is required to reach their summits. The individual will have to decide whether these tops should be included, but all but serious rock climbers will eventually have to escape leftwards when confronted by Veleta's summit crag. The road can be reached almost anywhere on the left, by descending over piled boulders and scree, and it can then be used to reach the Veleta col and the south-west ridge which leads easily up to the summit (see Route 43).

Now retrace your steps to the col and traverse the rocky crest of Tajos de la Virgen and Tajos del Neveros (Route 25) to the Elorrieta hut. The High Route makes a descent north-west from the col - following the red poles which mark the Olimpica ski run - to the Lagunillas de la Virgen, then picks up the good path to Elorrieta (Route 24), thus bypassing the Virgen/Neveros ridge.

At the Elorrieta hut, High Routers can look forward to a straightforward walk along the Vereda Cortada (see Route 27) to the foot of Cerro del Caballo, but die-hard Integral-ers face a long out and back detour to the summit of Tajos de los Machos (Route 26), followed by the rough traverse of Tosal de Cartujo and Tajos Altos (see Route 27) to reach the final 3000-er.

From Caballo it's all downhill, but the walk is not over yet; Lanjarón is still 14km distant and 2400m below. Refer to Route 33 for details of the descent route, but note that the path from the Ventura hut leads down to join one of the relatively new 4WD tracks on Caballo's south ridge. This will lead you down to Lanjarón, but is longer than the traditional descent via Casa Tello and the Camino de la Sierra.

APPENDIX A
USEFUL ADDRESSES

1. ALTITUD
   Guías de montaña
   Apartado de Correos 1230
   18080 - GRANADA
   (Tel. 958 285387)
   Guided walks in the Sierra
   Nevada and Alpujarras.

2. AUTOBUSES ALSINA
   GRAELLS
   Estacion de autobuses
   Camino de Ronda
   GRANADA
   (Tel. 958 251354)
   The major 'inter-city' coach
   operator. Buses between
   Granada and Almeria, Málaga,
   Guadix etc. Also services into
   the Alpujarras.

3. CAMPING LAS LOMAS
   Carretera Güéjar Sierra,
   Km 6
   GRANADA
   (Tel. 958 470742)
   Probably the best campsite in
   the area, though a little remote
   from Granada. Competitive
   rates, good facilities, shady
   pitches, swimming pool, bar,
   restaurant. Owner speaks a little
   English and likes to practise!
   This site is slightly cooler due to
   its 1000m altitude.

4. FEDERATION ANDALUZA
   DE MONTAÑISMO
   Camino de Ronda 101
   Edificio Atalaya, 1, 7 G
   18003 - GRANADA
   The main centre of information
   on the Sierra. The author's first
   port of call on his first visit to
   Granada.

5. NEVADENSIS S.C.A.
   Calle Verónica
   18411 Pampaneira
   (GRANADA)
   (Tel. 763127)
   A thriving guiding and
   environmental education
   business. Guided walks, trips
   on horseback, trips by 4WD
   vehicle and conservation
   education courses.

6. PATRONATO DE TURISMO
   Oficina de Informacion
   Plaza Mariana Pineda 10
   18009 - GRANADA
   (Tel. 958 223527)
   Tourist information. Much info
   on hotels, ski-resorts, bus
   services etc.

7. JUNTA DE ANDALUCIA,
   Dirección Provincial de la
   Agencia de Medio Ambiente
   de Granada
   Gran Vía de Colón,
   48 - 2 y 3 planta
   18010 - GRANADA
   The local 'Council for the
   Environment', controlling
   many aspects of access and
   conservation. The Junta can
   provide up to date information
   on fire risk in specific areas etc.
   Its vehicles are always much in
   evidence in the remote areas of
   the range.

APPENDIX B
THE LANGUAGE

Spanish is an extremely logical language. There are a few rules of pronunciation and grammar to be learned, but most people will soon gain sufficient grasp of these to be able to get by in Spain. Generally, the Spanish people are extremely helpful when it comes to assisting foreigners, and have great patience when trying to understand what you are trying to say.

It is not the purpose of this book to perform the function of a translator, but I have included a glossary of Spanish terms below. The glossary includes translations of some place names which will be found on the maps and in the text of this book, and also some Spanish terms which will be encountered by the traveller in the Sierra, either on notices or in local tourist literature. I have excluded some words which are so similar to their English equivalents that their meaning is obvious (e.g. dificil = difficult), and also words which are so well known that translation is unnecessary (e.g. gracias, adios). A rough guide to translation is bracketed where this might be useful.

GLOSSARY OF SPANISH TERMS

Abajo (a-BA-ho)	:	below, down, underneath
Abierto	:	open
Abrigo	:	shelter, protection
Acampada	:	camp (but often 'camping' is used instead)
Acequia	:	irrigation channel
Agua	:	water ('agua potable' = drinking water)
Aguila	:	eagle
Aguja (a-GOO-ha)	:	pinnacle, steeple, needle
Ahi (a-YI)	:	there
Ahora (a-O-ra)	:	now
Albergue	:	hostel, hut
Alcazaba	:	citadel, fortress
Alimento	:	food, nourishment
(de) Alquiler (al-KI-ler)	:	for hire
Alto	:	high
Alud	:	avalanche
Andar	:	walk, to travel on foot
Año (AN-yo)	:	year ('todo el año' = all year round)
Aparcamento	:	car park
Aqui (a-KI)	:	here
Arenal	:	sandy, sands
Arista	:	arête, sharp ridge

143

Arroyo	:	stream, watercourse
Atalaya	:	watchtower
Baja, Bajo (BA-ha, BA-ho)	:	low, lower
Barranco	:	ravine, gill
Barrio	:	quarter, district, suburb
Basura	:	rubbish, litter
Bienvenido	:	welcome
Blanquillo (blan-KI-yo)	:	whitish, white
Búho (BOO-o)	:	owl
Caballo (kab-A-yo)	:	horse
Cabra	:	goat
Cadena	:	chain, chain barrier
Caldera	:	cauldron
Caliente	:	hot
Calor	:	heat
Cambio	:	change
Camino	:	path, track
Camión	:	lorry
Campanario	:	bell tower
Cañada (kan-yada)	:	ravine, glen, canyon
Cañuto (kan-yuto)	:	pipe, gully
Carretera	:	road
Carril	:	lane, carriageway, rail
Casa	:	house
Cascajar (kas-ca-har)	:	scree slope
Castillejo (kastil-yeho)	:	scaffold, climbing frame
Castillo (kas-TEEl-yo)	:	castle
Cerrado (th-er-ado)	:	closed
Cerro (therro)	:	hill
Cerveza (ther-VAY-tha)	:	beer
Ciervo (thi-ervo)	:	stag
Circunvalación	:	bypass
Ciudad (thi-oodad)	:	city
Claro	:	clearly, clear
Collado (col-YADO)	:	depression between summits, col
Cortijo (kor-TI-ho)	:	farm
Creston	:	crest
Cuenta (kwenta)	:	count, the bill
Cuesta (kwesta)	:	slope, brow
Cueva (kwayva)	:	cave
Derecha	:	right (direction)
Descanso	:	rest
Deshielo (des-YAY-lo)	:	thaw, de-icing

Domingero	:	Sunday tripper ('domingo' = Sunday)
Erizo (e-REE-tho)	:	hedgehog
Ermita (er-MEE-ta)	:	hermitage
Escalar	:	to climb, scale
Este (es-ti)	:	east
Estrecha	:	narrow
Estrella (es-TREL-ya)	:	star
Facil (fa-thil)	:	easy
Ferrocarril	:	railway
Fuego (fwaygo)	:	fire
Hacer (ath-er)	:	to make
Hola (ola)	:	hello
Hoy (oy)	:	today
Hoya (oya)	:	valley, pit
Infierno (infyerno)	:	hell
Integral (integ-RAL)	:	whole, complete
Invierno (invi-yerno)	:	winter
Izquierda (ith-KEER-da)	:	left (direction)
Jardín (har-DIN)	:	garden
Jeres, Jerez (her-eth)	:	sherry
Loma	:	rib, ridge
Llano (YA-no)	:	flat
Mañana (man-YANA)	:	literally 'morning' but also means 'later'
Mata	:	shrub, bush
Merendero	:	snack bar
Mirador	:	view point
Mochila (motch-EELA)	:	rucksack
Mojón (mo-HON)	:	heap, cairn, also a boundary stone
Nevada	:	snowstorm, blizzard, snowy
Norte (nor-ti)	:	north
Nieve (ni-ayvi)	:	snow
Obra	:	work
Oeste (westi)	:	west
Otoño (o-TON-yo)	:	autumn
Oveja (o-VAY-ha)	:	sheep
Pared (pa-red)	:	wall
Paso	:	passage, way
Peligro	:	danger
Pelado, Pelada, Pelao	:	peeled, bald
Pescado, Pesca	:	fish
Pino	:	pine tree
Pozo (po-tho)	:	deep pool, well
Prado	:	meadow, pasture

Primavera	:	spring
Puente (pwenti)	:	bridge
Puerta, Puerto (pwerta)	:	door, major pass
Puntal	:	prop, support ('punta' = point, tip)
Que (ke)	:	what, which
Rambla	:	stream, watercourse
Raspa	:	scratch ('raspon' = big scratch)
Recuerde (rek-oo-erdi)	:	remember
Refugio, (ref-OO-hio)	:	hut, shelter
Salida (sal-EE-da)	:	exit
Seco	:	dry
Sierra	:	saw, mountains (from likeness to saw teeth)
Sud	:	south
Tiempo (tee-empo)	:	weather, time (depending on context)
Tienda (tee-enda)	:	tent, shop (depending on context)
Todo	:	all
Toma	:	take, taking
Vaca	:	cow
Veleta	:	weathercock
Ventisquero	:	snowpatch, snowdrift
Ventura	:	luck, fortune, happiness
Vereda	:	path
Veta (vayta)	:	vein, seam
Vía (vEEa)	:	way, route
Viaje (vee-aa-hi)	:	journey ('viajar' = to travel)
Vibora	:	viper
Vuelta (vwelta)	:	tour, circuit, lap
Yegua (yegwa)	:	mare
Zorro (thorro)	:	fox

APPENDIX C
BIBLIOGRAPHY

Other Walking Guides in Spanish

Andar por Sierra Nevada by Jorge Garzon Gutiérrez.

Contains 25 routes in low and medium mountains (up to 2500m), colour photographs, maps, diagrams and sketches.

A *Buho Viajero* ('owl guide') published by Acción Divulgativa, S.L., Enrique Velasco, 40, 28038 MADRID. (1992)

Andar por las Alpujarras by Agustín García Martínez.

Similar to the above but covering the Alpujarras.

Sierra Nevada Guia Montañera by Pablo Bueno Porcel.

The definitive Spanish guide. 65 routes, 8 maps, numerous photos in colour and black and white, some with climbing routes illustrated. 564 pages.

Latest edition published 1987 by Granada University, Campus Universitario de Cartuja, GRANADA.

Other Walking Guides in English

Gredos Mountains and Sierra Nevada by Robin Collomb.

Mostly devoted to Sierra de los Gredos. Gives only basic outline info on Sierra Nevada.

A *Guide Collomb* published by West Col Productions, Reading, Berks. RG8 9AA. (1987)

Other Books in Spanish

Rutas BH de Mountain Bike (Granada) by Alejandro Ortega.

25 bike-friendly routes in Sierra Nevada and surrounding area, sketch maps, route relief diagrams.

A *Rutas BH* guide, published by Ediciones Tutor, Sebastian Elcano, 30, 28012 MADRID.

La Aventura de Sierra Nevada 1717-1915 by Manuel Titos Martínez.

Historical accounts of the early 'excursionistas' explorations of the Sierra. Many interesting historic photographs, maps and diagrams.

Published in 1990 by Granada University, Campus Universitario de Cartuja, GRANADA.

Other Books in English

Wild Spain by Frederic V. Grunfeld.

General traveller's and naturalist's guide. Contains much good information on Spain's wild areas including Sierra Nevada.

Published in 1988 by Ebury Press, Colquhoun House, 27-37 Broadrick Street, London W1V 1FR.

Maps of the Sierra Nevada

1. Instituto Geográfico Nacional (IGN) at 1:25,000 scale.

Far below British O.S. standards, but the most accurate maps available. Footpath info very poor. Labelling dire. Cover south Granada and the Sierra in 9 sheets:

Armilla	(sht 1026-2)	Padul	(sht 1026-4)
Durcal	(sht 1041-2)	Güéjar Sierra	(sht 1027-1)
Veleta	(sht 1027-3)	Lanjarón	(sht 1042-2)
Picón Jeres	(sht 1027-2)	Trevélez	(sht 1042-4)
Bérchules	(sht 1042-2)		

Published by IGN, Sección de Cartografía, General Ibáñez de Ibero, 3, MADRID-3.

2. Servicio Geográfico del Ejército (SGE) at 1:50,000 scale.

Military maps. Now out of date in a number of important areas. Labelling better than IGN maps, but still confused in places. Cover the main area of the guide in 4 sheets:

Padul (19-42), Güéjar Sierra (20-42), Durcal (19-43), Lanjarón (20-43).

3. Federacíon Española de Montañismo (FEM) at 1:50,000 scale.

A very useful general planning map. Covers the whole guide area on one sheet. Shaded to give an impression of relief. Paths, tracks, roads information inaccurate in many areas. Also, crags marked where none exist, and vice versa. Reverse of sheet printed with much useful info on hotels, ski-resort, climbing areas, etc.

Map is titled *Sierra Nevada - Estacion Invernal y Alpujarras.*

Published by FEM, Alberto Aguilera 3, 4 Izquierda, MADRID-15.

In England

> Stanfords
> 27A Floral Street,
> London WC2E 9LP
> 0171 836 1321

> The Map Shop,
> 15 High Street,
> Upton-upon-Severn,Worcs
> WR8 OHJ
> 01684 593 146

stock all the maps plus smaller scale tourist maps of the area

CICERONE GUIDES

Cicerone publish a wide range of reliable guides to walking and climbing abroad

FRANCE, BELGIUM & LUXEMBOURG
CHAMONIX MONT BLANC - A Walking Guide
THE CORSICAN HIGH LEVEL ROUTE: GR20
FRENCH ROCK
THE PYRENEAN TRAIL: GR10
THE RLS (Stevenson) TRAIL
ROCK CLIMBS IN BELGIUM & LUXEMBOURG
ROCK CLIMBS IN THE VERDON
TOUR OF MONT BLANC
TOUR OF THE OISANS: GR54
TOUR OF THE QUEYRAS
WALKING THE FRENCH ALPS: GR5
WALKING THE FRENCH GORGES (Provence)
WALKS IN VOLCANO COUNTRY (Auvergne)
THE WAY OF ST JAMES: GR65

FRANCE / SPAIN
WALKS AND CLIMBS IN THE PYRENEES
ROCK CLIMBS IN THE PYRENEES

SPAIN & PORTUGAL
ANDALUSIAN ROCK CLIMBS
BIRDWATCHING IN MALLORCA
COSTA BLANCA CLIMBS
MOUNTAIN WALKS ON THE COSTA BLANCA
WALKING IN MALLORCA
WALKS & CLIMBS IN THE PICOS DE EUROPA
THE WAY OF ST JAMES: SPAIN
WALKING IN THE ALGARVE

FRANCE / SWITZERLAND
CHAMONIX TO ZERMATT The Walker's Haute Route
THE JURA - Walking the High Route and Winter Ski
    Traverses

SWITZERLAND
THE ALPINE PASS ROUTE
THE BERNESE ALPS
CENTRAL SWITZERLAND
THE GRAND TOUR OF MONTE ROSA (inc Italy)
WALKS IN THE ENGADINE
WALKING IN TICINO
THE VALAIS - A Walking Guide

GERMANY / AUSTRIA / EASTERN EUROPE
HUT-TO-HUT IN THE STUBAI ALPS
THE HIGH TATRAS
THE KALKALPEN TRAVERSE
KING LUDWIG WAY
KLETTERSTEIG - Scrambles
MOUNTAIN WALKING IN AUSTRIA
WALKING IN THE BLACK FOREST
WALKING IN THE HARZ MOUNTAINS
WALKING IN THE SALZKAMMERGUT

ITALY & SLOVENIA
ALTA VIA - High Level Walks in the Dolomites
CLASSIC CLIMBS IN THE DOLOMITES
THE GRAND TOUR OF MONTE ROSA (inc Switzerland))
ITALIAN ROCK - Rock Climbs in Northern Italy
VIA FERRATA - Scrambles in the Dolomites
WALKING IN THE DOLOMITES
WALKS IN THE JULIAN ALPS

MEDITERRANEAN COUNTRIES
THE ATLAS MOUNTAINS
CRETE: Off the beaten track
THE MOUNTAINS OF GREECE
THE MOUNTAINS OF TURKEY
TREKS & CLIMBS IN WADI RUM, JORDAN
THE ALA DAG - Climbs & Treks (Turkey)

OTHER COUNTRIES
ADVENTURE TREKS - W. N. AMERICA
ANNAPURNA TREKKERS GUIDE
CLASSIC TRAMPS IN NEW ZEALAND
MOUNTAIN WALKING IN AFRICA 1: KENYA
ROCK CLIMBS IN HONG KONG
TREKKING IN THE CAUCAUSUS
TREKKING IN NEPAL
TREKKING - WESTERN NORTH AMERICA

GENERAL OUTDOOR BOOKS
THE ADVENTURE ALTERNATIVE
FAMILY CAMPING
FIRST AID FOR HILLWALKERS
THE HILL WALKERS MANUAL
LIMESTONE -100 BEST CLIMBS IN BRITAIN
MOUNTAIN WEATHER
MOUNTAINEERING LITERATURE
MODERN ALPINE CLIMBING
MODERN SNOW & ICE TECHNIQUES
ROPE TECHNIQUES IN MOUNTAINEERING

CANOEING
CANOEIST'S GUIDE TO THE NORTH EAST
SNOWDONIA WILD WATER, SEA & SURF
WILDWATER CANOEING

CARTOON BOOKS
ON FOOT & FINGER
ON MORE FEET & FINGERS
LAUGHS ALONG THE PENNINE WAY
THE WALKERS

*Also a full range of guidebooks
to walking, scrambling, ice-climbing,
rock climbing, and other adventurous
pursuits in Britain and abroad*

*Other guides are constantly being added to the Cicerone List.
Available from bookshops, outdoor equipment shops or direct (send for price list)
from CICERONE, 2 POLICE SQUARE, MILNTHORPE, CUMBRIA, LA7 7PY*

CICERONE GUIDES
Cicerone publish a wide range of reliable guides to walking and climbing in Britain, and other general interest books.

LAKE DISTRICT - General Books
CONISTON COPPER A History
CHRONICLES OF MILNTHORPE
A DREAM OF EDEN
THE HIGH FELLS OF LAKELAND
LAKELAND - A taste to remember (Recipes)
LAKELAND VILLAGES
LAKELAND TOWNS
THE LOST RESORT? (Morecambe)
LOST LANCASHIRE (Furness area)
OUR CUMBRIA Stories of Cumbrian Men and Women
THE PRIORY OF CARTMEL
REFLECTIONS ON THE LAKES
AN ILLUSTRATED COMPANION INTO LAKELAND

LAKE DISTRICT - Guide Books
THE BORDERS OF LAKELAND
BIRDS OF MORECAMBE BAY
CASTLES IN CUMBRIA
CONISTON COPPER MINES Field Guide
THE CUMBRIA CYCLE WAY
THE EDEN WAY
IN SEARCH OF WESTMORLAND
SHORT WALKS IN LAKELND-1: SOUTH LAKELAND
SCRAMBLES IN THE LAKE DISTRICT
MORE SCRAMBLES IN THE LAKE DISTRICT
WALKING ROUND THE LAKES
WALKS IN SILVERDALE/ARNSIDE
WESTMORLAND HERITAGE WALK
WINTER CLIMBS IN THE LAKE DISTRICT

NORTHERN ENGLAND (outside the Lakes
BIRDWATCHING ON MERSEYSIDE
CANAL WALKS Vol 1 North
CANOEISTS GUIDE TO THE NORTH EAST
THE CLEVELAND WAY & MISSING LINK
THE DALES WAY
DOUGLAS VALLEY WAY
WALKING IN THE FOREST OF BOWLAND
HADRIANS WALL Vol 1 The Wall Walk
HERITAGE TRAILS IN NW ENGLAND
THIE ISLE OF MAN COASTAL PATH
IVORY TOWERS & DRESSED STONES (Follies)
THE LANCASTER CANAL
LANCASTER CANAL WALKS
A WALKERS GUIDE TO THE LANCASTER CANAL
LAUGHS ALONG THE PENNINE WAY
A NORTHERN COAST-TO-COAST
NORTH YORK MOORS Walks
THE REIVERS WAY (Northumberland)
THE RIBBLE WAY
ROCK CLIMBS LANCASHIRE & NW
WALKING DOWN THE LUNE
WALKING IN THE SOUTH PENNINES
WALKING IN THE NORTH PENNINES
WALKING IN THE WOLDS
WALKS IN THE YORKSHIRE DALES (3 VOL)
WALKS IN LANCASHIRE WITCH COUNTRY
WALKS IN THE NORTH YORK MOORS
WALKS TO YORKSHIRE WATERFALLS (2 vol)
WATERFALL WALKS -TEESDALE & THE HIGH PENNINES
WALKS ON THE WEST PENNINE MOORS
WALKING NORTHERN RAILWAYS (2 vol)
THE YORKSHIRE DALES A walker's guide

Also a full range of EUROPEAN and OVERSEAS guidebooks - walking, long distance trails, scrambling, ice-climbing, rock climbing.

DERBYSHIRE & EAST MIDLANDS
KINDER LOG
HIGH PEAK WALKS
WHITE PEAK WAY
WHITE PEAK WALKS - 2 Vols
WEEKEND WALKS IN THE PEAK DISTRICT
THE VIKING WAY
THE DEVIL'S MILL / WHISTLING CLOUGH (Novels)

WALES & WEST MIDLANDS
ASCENT OF SNOWDON
WALKING IN CHESHIRE
CLWYD ROCK
HEREFORD & THE WYE VALLEY A Walker's Guide
HILLWALKING IN SNOWDONIA
HILL WALKING IN WALES (2 Vols)
THE MOUNTAINS OF ENGLAND & WALES Vol 1 WALES
WALKING OFFA'S DYKE PATH
THE RIDGES OF SNOWDONIA
ROCK CLIMBS IN WEST MIDLANDS
SARN HELEN Walking Roman Road
SCRAMBLES IN SNOWDONIA
SNOWDONIA WHITE WATER SEA & SURF
THE SHROPSHIRE HILLS A Walker's Guide
WALKING DOWN THE WYE
WELSH WINTER CLIMBS

SOUTH & SOUTH WEST ENGLAND
WALKING IN THE CHILTERNS
COTSWOLD WAY
COTSWOLD WALKS (3 VOLS)
WALKING ON DARTMOOR
WALKERS GUIDE TO DARTMOOR PUBS
EXMOOR & THE QUANTOCKS
THE KENNET & AVON WALK
LONDON THEME WALKS
AN OXBRIDGE WALK
A SOUTHERN COUNTIES BIKE GUIDE
THE SOUTHERN-COAST-TO-COAST
SOUTH DOWNS WAY & DOWNS LINK
SOUTH WEST WAY - 2 Vol
THE TWO MOORS WAY Dartmoor-Exmoor
WALKS IN KENT Bk 2
THE WEALDWAY & VANGUARD WAY

SCOTLAND
THE BORDER COUNTRY - WALKERS GUIDE
BORDER PUBS & INNS A Walker's Guide
CAIRNGORMS WINTER CLIMBS
WALKING THE GALLOWAY HILLS
THE ISLAND OF RHUM
THE SCOTTISH GLENS (Mountainbike Guide)
   Book 1:THE CAIRNGORM GLENS
   Book 2 THE ATHOLL GLENS
   Book 3 THE GLENS OF RANNOCH
SCOTTISH RAILWAY WALKS
SCRAMBLES :N LOCHABER
SCRAMBLES IN SKYE
SKI TOURING IN SCOTLAND
TORRIDON A Walker's Guide
WALKS from the WEST HIGHLAND RAILWAY
WINTER CLIMBS BEN NEVIS & GLENCOE

REGIONAL BOOKS UK & IRELAND
THE ALTERNATIVE PENNINE WAY
CANAL WALKS Vol.1: North
LIMESTONE - 100 BEST CLIMBS
THE PACKHORSE BRIDGES OF ENGLAND
THE RELATIVE HILLS OF BRITAIN
THE MOUNTAINS OF ENGLAND & WALES
   VOL 1 WALES, VOL 2 ENGLAND
THE MOUNTAINS OF IRELAND

Other guides are constantly being added to the Cicerone List.
Available from bookshops, outdoor equipment shops or direct (send s.a.e. for price list) from
CICERONE, 2 POLICE SQUARE, MILNTHORPE, CUMBRIA, LA7 7PY

PRINTED BY CARNMOR PRINT & DESIGN, LONDON ROAD, PRESTON, LANCS.